Toward a new era in
ARTS
EDUCATION

Edited by JOHN T. MCLAUGHLIN

Toward a new era in ARTS EDUCATION

Interlochen Symposium

The Interlochen Symposium was co-convened by the American Council for the Arts and Music Educators National Conference and was underwritten by the generous support of the Interlochen Arts Center, the National Endowment for the Arts, and the Sears-Roebuck Foundation.

Edited by Barbara Ryan
Book and jacket design by Celine Brandes, Photo Plus Art

Typesetting by Creative Graphics
Printing by Bookcrafters

Director of Publishing: Robert Porter
Assistant Director of Publishing: Amy Jennings

Library of Congress Cataloging-in-Publication Data

Toward a new era in arts education.

    Bibliography: p.
    Includes index.
    1. Arts—Study and teaching—United States
—Congresses. I. McLaughlin, John, 1953-.
NX303.T69   1988   700'.7'1073   88-16649

ISBN 0-915400-69-3

This publication was made possible
by the generous support of the
Sears-Roebuck Foundation

CONTENTS

ACKNOWLEDGMENTS

A three-day event such as the Interlochen Symposium depends upon the cooperation of many people and organizations, and this is an opportune moment to thank those who gave careful and attentive consideration to every detail, both philosophical and logistical.

Three committees, in particular, deserve special recognition: the Ad Hoc National Arts Education Working Group, the American Council for the Arts' Education Committee, and the Interlochen Symposium Content Committee. Each of these groups made invaluable contributions in shaping the symposium and in the decision-making process used to select the topics for the discussion papers. Notably representing these groups, Milton Rhodes, ACA president, John Mahlmann, Music Educators National Conference executive director, Fred Lazarus IV, Ad Hoc National Arts Education Working Group chairman, and John Straus, ACA Arts Education Committee chairman, all deserve special mention for their insight and advice throughout the two years of planning and preparation for this project.

Much appreciation is extended to James Cape, former associate director of development at Interlochen, without whose initial assistance the Interlochen Symposium would have never been a reality. And no words are sufficient to thank Roger Jacobi, president of the Interlochen Arts Center, and his staff for all of their efforts in making sure that the participants were adequately housed, fed, entertained and transported to and from the airport. Much of the credit for this hard work goes to Donna Shugart, director of special events at Interlochen, and her assistants, Amy Diment and Reed Coombs. Rosalyn Ridgway, director of public affairs, and Patti DiAgostino, director of the news bureau, worked diligently to assure great media coverage of the events. Interlochen's in-house photographers, Wayne and Mary Brill, covered the symposium and are responsible for all the photographs in this book. Video coverage was provided by David Greenspan.

Much appreciation is due Barbara Goldman, executive director of the Michigan Council for the Arts, and her staff for helping to arrange the Traverse City events and for serving as ambassadors of goodwill from Michigan. The generous hospitality of Terry Tarnow, Traverse City Arts Council director, and of Reed Zitting, Traverse City Opera House manager, was greatly valued. Finally, the Interlochen students provided excellent entertainment and willingly answered participants' questions about the program of the Interlochen Academy.

Peggy Sullivan of MENC spent many hours on the telephone efficiently and cheerfully answering the most minute of questions and assuring smooth cooperation between ACA and MENC on this project. Also, a special thanks to Mary Ann Cameron for her efforts in handling the publicity from MENC.

The dedicated staff of professionals at ACA provided valuable and much-needed support. Sarah Havens, executive director, did an exemplary job of handling ACA's public relations. Robert Porter, director of publishing, and his assistant, Amy Jennings, helped condense two years of planning and a four-day event into this book. Barbara Rubin, an ACA national patron, wandered into the ACA office one cold winter day and stayed to provide valuable assistance in keeping the process on track. Finally, a very special thanks to Tom Becker, assistant arts education director, for his unfailing and uncomplaining dedication to the countless tasks required to prepare and conduct the symposium.

Finally, a special debt of gratitude is due to the participants who discussed, who thought, who planned and who dreamed in order to move this field *Toward a New Era in Arts Education*.

This book is dedicated to Charles McWhorter for his unwavering support of this project, from its inception at the President's Committee meeting to its execution over the four days in November.

J.T.M.

1
The Process

TOWARD THE NEXT DECADE

We have just passed 1987, a landmark year in America's short history, during which our celebration of the drafting of the Constitution brought to a close our remembrance of the nation's bicentennial, which began in 1976. These have been years when, once again, Americans have reflected on the values and achievements that constitute American civilization.

The arts, the teaching of the arts, and the learning of the arts are basic to broadening and deepening the culture that supports everything we do as a nation. While the importance of the arts and arts education are too often underestimated, their influence or lack thereof shapes our society and the capabilities of our people as surely as evolving economic, political or religious conditions. Given this powerful influence, how are we doing; how successful have we been at developing the cultural foundations for our future?

To begin answering, we can state unequivocally that our nation has large numbers of talented, capable, and dedicated individuals involved professionally in the arts and in teaching the arts. When the importance of their mission is understood and supported at the local level, they produce results that are the envy of the entire world. Fortunately, such support is available in numerous situations, and the results are evident in outstanding artistic and educational achievements. In the aggregate, these situations provide the impetus for the artistic development of American civilization. They yield the artists, the works of art, and the knowledgeable audiences that sustain our cultural advancement. Why, then, should there be cause for concern?

The last five years have been full of debate about the role that the arts and arts education should play in elementary and secondary education. In all fields, anxieties have arisen about the ability of our current education system to sustain the values and develop the capabilities necessary for the maintenance of our nation's productivity and leadership in the years ahead. After many national reports and much discussion, one general conclusion has emerged: Excellence

exists, but not in sufficient quantity. The same can be said for arts education specifically. There are outstanding programs, but there are simply not enough of them. Too few students gain the basic knowledge and skills that will enable them to deal with the arts as matters of the mind—a condition we cannot afford to accept for a set of disciplines so basic to our civilization.

The arts and the teaching of the arts exert major influences on society. Likewise, economic, social, political, and other trends influence the arts and arts education. Values change over time, and among those with decision-making powers, changing values produce conflicting views of relative worth. Solutions aimed at large problems often have unforeseen adverse effects. These and other conditions are not unique to arts education, but their presence is often magnified in this field because neither the arts nor arts education has been given the priority each deserves in American life. The result, for the arts field as a whole, has been continual economic difficulties and the unhealthy internal tensions which economic anxieties provoke. Further, these anxieties provide fertile conceptual ground for shifting from a set of basic values in which the arts, arts education, and civilization are inextricably linked to a foundation based on unilateral faith in survival techniques. Methods of fundraising and delivering services become ends rather than means, coordination diminishes, and basic goals become obscured. Most of the conditions that affect arts education adversely—from within and from without—can be traced to this root problem or to one of its many manifestations.

Leaders in the arts and arts education have increasingly realized that this means/ends confusion is a major obstruction to the expansion of excellent school-based teaching and learning in the arts. And this realization has led to an organized effort to re-establish a common conceptual base through comprehensive examination of the critical issues.

To begin, the American Council for the Arts (ACA) and Music Educators National Conference (MENC) convened over 30 leaders from arts education associations, arts advocacy groups, and arts service organizations for a day-long discussion. This meeting, held at the  Philadelphia office of the Pew Memorial Trust on March 24, 1986, put many of the key issues on the table for consideration.

There in Philadelphia, we reaffirmed that common cause is more important than organizational differences. We also found that one meeting was not enough. The representatives of the 31 organizations present agreed to convene again in May, and since that time they have met frequently. They are currently known as the Ad Hoc National Arts Education Working Group.

At the first meeting, the group drafted the "Philadelphia Resolution," a document which expresses consensus on common values in arts education. After the text was refined at the next meeting, the individual members of the group took the revised document to the boards of their respective organizations for adoption.

Next came the drafting of a second document to establish operational principles based on a value statement contained in the "Philadelphia Resolution." This 11-point document, "Concepts for Strengthening Arts Education in Schools," puts forth specific guidelines for the improvement of arts education that can be applied to every aspect of the schooling process.

Taken together, these two documents could serve as an excellent starting point for local communities working to improve arts education in their schools. The texts of the "Philadelphia Resolution" and "Concepts for Strengthening Arts Education in Schools," along with the list of organizations participating in the Ad Hoc National Arts Education Working Group, follow this article.

In addition to producing these documents, the group has addressed several specific concerns in arts education as they evolved. For example, the group worked to assure that the arts were mentioned in the report on elementary education prepared by United

States Secretary of Education William Bennett. In the report, *First Lessons*, which appeared in September 1986, the arts were included in the basic curriculum, as explained in the following statement:

The arts are essential elements of education just like reading, writing, and arithmetic. . . . Music, dance, painting, and theater are keys that unlock profound human understanding and accomplishment. Children should be handed these keys at an early age.

Several members of the Ad Hoc National Arts Education Working Group participated as panelists or observers in hearings held by the National Endowment for the Arts during preparation of a report on the state of arts education, the first study in this area mandated by Congress in almost 100 years. Ideas from the "Philadelphia Resolution" and our "Concepts" paper are reflected in the final report, entitled *Toward Civilization*. In the process of convening the Interlochen Symposium, ACA and MENC consulted the Ad Hoc Arts

 Education Working Group. Some of the group served on the content committee, which composed the symposium papers and served in an advisory capacity for the design of the symposium. This relationship of the group to the evolving symposium assured that what happened over the three days at Interlochen would encourage all the participants involved in arts education to work together at local, regional, and national levels.

The symposium is over now, and much needs to be done. Interlochen produced 32 specific recommendations for improving arts education. Among them was the call for a group to serve as a national forum on arts education, and continuation of the Ad Hoc National Arts Education Working Group seems the logical venue for carrying out this mandate. We are pleased that this national collaborative venture will continue, and we hope that the spirit of collaboration for the improvement of arts education pervades the entire country. Where there has been collaboration, efforts to improve arts education often have enjoyed increased productivity.

History shows, however, that collaboration must be based on

principles that produce substantive results. Collaboration must be a means of strengthening the work of those who go into the schools daily and teach the arts, not simply an end in itself. Since improvement on the national level depends on an aggregation of local successes, we must focus now on increasing what students know and are able to do in the arts. We must accomplish this student by student, class by class, school by school, district by district. Our analysis reveals that this mission of substance is our primary challenge for the next decade. In 1998, we want to look back on ten years of significant progress as manifest in documented student achievement.

We hope that the following texts, which stimulated us at Interlochen, will help you work toward this goal wherever you are and whatever you do. We also hope that you will share your ideas and concerns with the Ad Hoc National Arts Education Working Group as this body strives to carry out its efforts in support of local teachers and students in the months and years ahead.

Milton Rhodes, President
American Council for the Arts

John Mahlmann, Executive Director
Music Educators National Conference

PHILADELPHIA RESOLUTION
March 24, 1986

WHEREAS, American Society is deeply concerned with the condition of elementary and secondary education; and

WHEREAS, the arts are basic to education and have great value in and of themselves and for the knowledge, skills and values they impart; and

WHEREAS, the arts are a widely neglected curriculum and educational resource in American schools; and

WHEREAS, numerous national reports have cited the arts as one of the most basic disciplines of the curriculum; and

WHEREAS, every American child should have equal educational opportunity to study the arts as representations of the highest intellectual achievements of humankind;

THEREFORE, the undersigned individuals, representing a broad cross-section of national arts organizations, agree:

THAT EVERY elementary and secondary school should offer a balanced, sequential, and high quality program of instruction in arts disciplines taught by qualified teachers and strengthened by artists and arts organizations as an essential component of the curriculum;

THAT WE PROMOTE public understanding of the connections between the study of the arts disciplines, the creation of art, and the development of a vibrant, productive American civilization;

THAT WE URGE inclusion of support for rigorous, comprehensive arts education in the arts development efforts of each community;

THAT WE PURSUE development of local, state and national policies that result in more effective support for arts education and the professional teachers and artists who provide it.

CONCEPTS FOR STRENGTHENING
ARTS EDUCATION IN SCHOOLS

To increase the level of artistic literacy in the nation as a whole, the arts must be taught with the same rigor, passion and commitment with which they are created and presented to the public. The primary responsibility to educate students rests with teachers, school administrators, and ultimately, local school boards who represent the public. But we all have a stake in this undertaking: artists, arts organizations, professional and community schools of art, arts teachers and administrators, those who teach the next generation of artists and teachers, and all those who believe the arts should be an integral part of people's lives.

We will work to establish the arts as an equal partner in the educational enterprise. The arts and arts education communities define common goals and discover the role each will play to further a vision of the future that includes the arts at the center of American values and practice.

Together, we advance these philosophical and operational concepts:

1. The arts should be taught as disciplines to all students. This includes student involvement in creating, studying, and experiencing the arts.

2. Regular instruction in the various arts must be a basic part of the curriculum in all elementary and secondary schools; such instruction must be integrated with the highest quality arts experiences both in schools and in theatres, concert halls, and museums; such experiences must be integrated with instruction as part of comprehensive curricula.

3. Arts curricula should be for the development of skills and knowledge of the arts. In addition, learning about and experiencing the arts can develop critical and creative thinking and perceptual abilities that extend to all areas of life. These benefits are best imparted through instruction in the basic skills in and knowledge of the arts.

4. The arts relate naturally to much of the content of the total educational curricula. For this reason, all teachers should

be encouraged to incorporate arts skills and knowledge into their instruction in order to enliven, broaden, and enrich all learning.

5. The curricula of teacher education programs in general should have a stronger arts component as part of the pedagogical preparation of all teachers.

6. Pre-service and in-service training of both teachers and artists should be augmented to include significantly greater experience of one another's working methods. Arts education benefits when arts teachers have high levels of artistic skill and knowledge of the arts, and when artists develop teaching abilities and knowledge of child development.

7. Resources are often available through individuals and arts organizations and in elementary, secondary, and postsecondary education to form the foundation for quality arts education programs in each local community. These resources must be identified, integrated, utilized and expanded.

8. The local focus for decision-making about arts services and arts education, including local control over curricula, must be respected. Within this framework, ways must be found at the local level to meet or exceed the goals and standards established by professional arts education associations and accreditation authorities. This should include criteria for school programs, certification of personnel, the participation of arts organizations, and artist and teacher preparation programs.

9. Arts education programs, which are designed to increase cultural literacy, will build audiences and strengthen community volunteer and funding support for cultural, visual and performing arts organizations and institutions. Therefore, these organizations should allocate significant resources and efforts in support of arts education.

10. We must establish for arts education a coordinated policy-making process that includes the arts and arts education

communities. Over time, this will vastly increase our ability to affect the policies of others whose support is needed to make the arts and the study of the arts more central to the educational mission of communities throughout the country.

11. Basic research, model projects, and advocacy efforts are critical to establishing a consistent and compelling case for increasing the economic base of support for arts education in schools and in the community at large. While the primary responsibility for increasing budget allocations in support of education programs rests with local school boards and administrators, we all must recognize our share in this responsibility as members of the larger society. We must build a powerful community constituency at local, state and national levels among arts and arts education organizations to initiate a step-by-step process for change.

PARTICIPATING ORGANIZATIONS

Alliance for Arts Education
Alliance of Independent Colleges of Art
American Association of Museums
American Alliance for Theatre and
Education
American Council for the Arts
American Dance Guild
American Symphony Orchestra League
The College Music Society
Dance/USA
High Fidelity/Musical America
International Council of Fine Arts Deans
Kennedy Center Education Program
Maryland Institute College of Fine Arts
Music Educators National Conference
National Art Education Association
National Assembly of Local Arts Agencies
National Assembly of State Arts Agencies
National Association of Jazz Educators
National Association of
Schools of Art and Design
National Association of Schools of Dance
National Association of Schools of Music
National Association of Schools of Theatre
National Band Association
National Dance Association
National Guild of
Community Schools of Art
National Music Council
Opera America
State Arts Advocacy League
Very Special Arts
Young Audiences

John McLaughlin

BUILDING CONSENSUS

T he days in the woods that became known as the Interlochen
Symposium have ended. Those who were involved—the participants, the content committee who assisted in the creation and the final shaping of the symposium, and the staffs of the Interlochen Arts Center, Music Educators National Conference, and the American Council for the Arts—can point with pride to a successful three days of discussions. Perhaps the recommendations that came out of the symposium, the formal and informal alliances formed among groups and individuals, and the theories explored in the six papers can truly move this diverse field *Toward a New Era in Arts Education.*

LAYING THE FOUNDATION

In retrospect, the two- to three-year process leading up to those three days in the woods, a somewhat bumpy journey at best, reflects the same themes that emerged during the symposium itself. These themes include coalition building and the bringing together  of diverse groups and individuals involved with arts education who had not spoken among themselves for many years, if at all. Finally, the development process is the story of our efforts to convince funders of the validity of a project that, although it did not promise a high-visibility product, would help to lay the groundwork for a better future for America's students. These themes deserve a few pages in this retelling to show how the process leading to the Interlochen Symposium actually became an integral part of the results and the overall effect.

The story begins at a 1985 meeting of the President's Commit-

tee on the Arts and Humanities. Because arts education was becoming an increasingly important concern in the arts and education fields, a major topic of discussion that day was the need to convene a large conference on arts education. Later, a small group of committee members got together to discuss the possible shape of such a meeting. This small group persuaded the Wallace Funds to sponsor a feasibility meeting at their offices in New York, a meeting which brought together a diverse group of individuals to examine the needs of the field and the critical issues that the arts education community must face in order to bring about long-range improvement. A number of decisions made at this meeting eventually would lead to the Interlochen Symposium:

1. Since the Interlochen Center for the Arts had demonstrated an ongoing commitment to excellence in the teaching of the arts to students, and since the center had conducted studies and seminars on various issues in arts education, it was decided that Interlochen would be an excellent site for a conference. Charles McWhorter, a member of the original discussion group and of the Interlochen board of directors, proved to be the primary mover in this decision.

2. A small group drawn from this committee was assigned the task of writing a proposal for the conference and sending it out to potential funders. The time frame at this point was the spring of 1986 (this would be changed many times). The design of the conference was to be geared primarily to teachers.

3. Milton Rhodes, president of the American Council for the Arts (ACA), and John Mahlmann, executive director of Music Educators National Conference (MENC), identified a need to bring together leaders in the arts education field from advocacy organizations, arts education associations, and professional associations to discuss common concerns

in the field, how these groups could work together to promote arts education, and how past differences among the organizations and individuals might be forgotten. This decision led to a meeting in Philadelphia, in March 1986, and to the formation of the Ad Hoc National Arts Education Working Group.

Progress at this point became slow. The Writing Committee came up with a proposal, *The Interlochen Symposium: The Fourth R*, which was shaped and reworked and sent out to a number of potential funders; but by the time the Ad Hoc Group met for the first time, the proposal had been rejected by all the major funders that had reviewed it. The reasons for rejection varied: some funders felt the symposium would be too expensive; most were not interested in funding symposia; some were not convinced of the need for another arts education meeting; others wondered what purpose would be served by a gathering of only 150 teachers. It was clear that the symposium as proposed had little chance of becoming a reality. In April 1986, Milton Rhodes agreed that ACA would rewrite the proposal before resuming the search for funding. This became one of the ongoing arts education projects of John McLaughlin, ACA's newly appointed director of arts education.

In rewriting the proposal, ACA had to confront several key issues:

1. Are teachers to be the primary participants in this symposium, or is there a need to reach a broader audience of decision makers?

2. Should this be a how-to workshop, or should it be a symposium in the purest sense of the word, with participants discussing and addressing key policy issues in arts education?

3. Should the symposium consist of one presentation after another by noted national experts, or was it time that profes-

sionals in the field came together and were given time to
share their own expertise and opinions?

4. Finally, how did the new Ad Hoc National Arts Education
Working Group fit into the process since it showed every
sign of building unity among the groups involved?

The questions began to be answered in ACA's discussions
with past and present leaders in the arts education field and with
members of the Ad Hoc Committee. First, those to whom the
questions were posed felt that the purposes of the symposium
would best be served by a broad representation of professionals in
the field. Second, rather than function as a how-to workshop, the
symposium should address key issues and collect the thoughts of
those active in many different aspects of the field. Third, the
agenda should not be overloaded; participants should be given
time to discuss ideas, share opinions, and make recommendations.

 It was also suggested that a number of key
position papers should be prepared to
serve as the starting point for discussions.
During July 1986, the revised proposal
was sent to new funders. The timeline for
conducting the symposium was now the
spring of 1987. *The Interlochen Symposium: Toward A New Era In
Arts Education* was drastically different from the original proposal,
but again funders were slow to respond. Like those who had received the original proposal, recipients of the revision appeared re-
luctant to fund a symposium even though the cost was only about
one-fifth that of the original. Then, in the fall of 1986, at a joint
meeting in Georgetown of ACA and MENC, the first positive light
shone on the enterprise. MENC had received a grant for a conference from the National Endowment for the Arts, but so far the
group had not been able to use the grant; they wondered if the
Arts Endowment would approve using the money for the Interlochen Symposium. Through the efforts of Joe Prince, then-direc-
tor of the National Endowment's Arts in Education program, the
authorization was granted. Again, the successful alliance of ACA

and MENC, which had brought about the Ad Hoc Group, became the convening alliance for the Interlochen Symposium.

Two steps remained to be taken: completion of the funding package and development of a realistic design based upon the proposal. It was now January of 1987, and once more the symposium would have to be postponed so that these two monumental tasks could be accomplished. In discussions with the Interlochen Center for the Arts, it was decided that the symposium would take place during the first weekend of November 1987 to avoid the conventions of major groups slated for the fall. Finally, a date had been set, and a symposium coordinator, John McLaughlin, appointed.

In a series of meetings with Jim Cape, Interlochen's assistant development director at the time, it was agreed that Interlochen would solicit in-kind contributions to cover housing, ground transportation, meals, audio and video taping, and other general support services. Negotiations with Interlochen were completed early in the spring; and in meetings in July with Robert Buzbee, national manager of the Sears-Roebuck Foundation, the foundation agreed to provide the final funding component.

The final symposium design was more difficult to complete than the funding. The decisions that led to the selection of a con-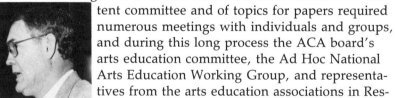tent committee and of topics for papers required numerous meetings with individuals and groups, and during this long process the ACA board's arts education committee, the Ad Hoc National Arts Education Working Group, and representatives from the arts education associations in Reston, Virginia, were frequently consulted. Although ultimately the process proved productive, at times these multiple perspectives were confusing and contradictory; each party seemed to have its own agenda. But at last, after months of discussions, six topics were identified and a 12-person content (steering) committee was selected, its membership carefully balanced between the academic world of arts education and actual practitioners from the arts

 professions and the educational commu-
nity. (Committee members are listed, with
brief biographies, in the appendix.) Each of
the six papers, it was decided, would be
co-written by a team of two, to incorporate
different points of view.

The committee, joined by Milton Rhodes, John Mahlmann,
John Straus and Charles McWhorter, met on March 17, 1987, at
the offices of Gannett Outdoor in New York City. Enthusiasm ran
high throughout the day-long meeting, during which careful
thought was given to the goals of the symposium. It was agreed
that the focus should be on how to assure that national theory,
policy, and research have the most positive effect possible on arts
education in local communities. Under McLaughlin's chairman-
ship, the group arrived at a number of key decisions affecting the
symposium's final shape:

1. In addition to the opinions of the writers, each paper would
   incorporate current theory and research on the assigned
   topic along with a series of questions to be discussed by the
   participants after the presentation. The papers would address a broad audience of decision makers and practitioners. The definition of local emphasis of arts education
   would be interpreted broadly to include, where appropriate, those states in which the state or regional level functions as the local level. The diverse needs of urban and
   rural education would be addressed as well. In the course
   of the meeting, the topics to be assigned to individual writing teams were refined into the form which appears in the
   next section of this book.

2. Papers would not be read at the symposium. Instead, they
   would be mailed to participants a month in advance. At the
   symposium, each paper would be the focus of a separate
   90-minute session. Following a ten-minute introduction by
   the co-writers, the balance of each session would be devoted to discussion of the questions contained in the paper.

3. Since the papers would reflect the opinions of the writers, it was decided that the manuscripts would not be rewritten during the symposium; rather, from the questions raised and the discussions provoked by those questions, a set of recommendations would be developed for each topic. Prior to the symposium, however, and before the papers would be sent to participants, the content committee would have an opportunity to review them, to make comments, and to call for revisions based on feedback from peers.

4. Symposium participants would be divided into ten groups of 15 each. Each participant would stay with the same group for all three sessions on the first day and then join another group for the three sessions on the second day. This arrangement, the committee felt, would give ample opportunity for different types of group dynamics.

5. The invitation process was to begin in June with the forwarding of letters of invitation to the organizations selected for representation at the symposium. The term "broad universe" became the operant consideration in choosing the actual participants. The content committee urged that, although the initial letters should go to presidents and chief executive officers, each organization should nominate its prospective representatives from among those most responsible and qualified in the area of arts education. Actual invitations would be mailed to those whose names were returned from this initial survey.

Also at the March meeting, the committee set deadlines for first drafts of the papers, for the return of comment sheets from participants, and for the completion of final manuscripts. The question of whether or not the symposium should feature a keynote speaker was discussed as well.

The following groups were considered for representation at the symposium:

- arts education associations
- arts professional organizations

- arts advocacy groups
- arts service organizations
- education associations
- minority organizations
- corporations and foundations with interest and programs in arts education
- eight of the states from the Arts Endowment's first group of Arts in Schools Basic Education grants
- media representatives

The invitation process was slow and arduous, and it was not completed until the last few weeks preceding the symposium. But after countless phone calls and follow-up letters, the organizers felt that their final list of participants (see appendix) was a true representation of the broad universe that the committee had sought from the beginning. Excluding the eight Arts Endowment states, approximately 70 organizations were considered in the initial stages of the invitation process. Invitations for the Arts En-  dowment states were sent to the arts education coordinators of the state arts agencies as well as to the arts coordinators at state departments of education. The participants ultimately selected included artists, educators, academics, and practitioners in arts education; they represented a wide geographic and demographic dispersion, and their organizations were national, state, and local. Many participants wore more than one hat; in addition to representing a university as a dean or a department head, they served as presidents of national organizations.

Apart from logistical glitches that were only to be expected in getting 150 people from all over the country to a small airport somewhere in the woods of Michigan, the last months of preparation went smoothly. The stage was finally set for the three days in the woods.

ACHIEVING ACCORD

November 5, 1987, began as a somewhat cool, yet sunny fall day. Final preparations were completed in the morning as participants began to arrive. By early evening, everyone had arrived, and at 7:30 p.m. they assembled on the stage of the concert hall for the opening dinner. Roger Jacobi, president of the Interlochen Arts Center, welcomed the group and briefly described the center. At that time, the Interlochen Arts Academy had an enrollment of 430 students representing 42 states and 12 foreign countries. Students in grades 9-12 pursue majors in music, creative writing, theater, visual arts, and set design and production. The National Music Camp, which operates during the summer, serves 2,500 students with a faculty and staff of 1,000.

Jacobi then introduced Charles McWhorter, trustee of Interlochen and president of the board of the American Ballet Theatre. He welcomed the group and then introduced Milton Rhodes, president of the American Council for the Arts, and John Mahlmann, executive director of Music Educators National Conference. Rhodes and Mahlmann recounted their efforts to bring the diverse fields of arts education represented at the symposium to agreement. As a prime example of how diverse professionals can work together for a common purpose, they pointed to the Ad Hoc National Arts Ed- ucation Working Group and its production of "The Philadelphia Resolution" and "Concepts for Strengthening Arts Education in Schools."

Following Rhodes and Mahlmann, seven of the participants outlined their expectations for the symposium. Brief summaries of their remarks follow.

Chris Van Antwerp (Michigan Association of Community Arts Organizations) emphasized the slowness of educational change and the need to help school boards, administrators, and teachers feel comfortable with the arts. His primary interests were learning how change can be effected in school districts, examining the role of local arts agencies, and determining how best to develop new leadership for the arts on school boards.

Richard Pioli (Montgomery County, Maryland, Public Schools) expressed his hope that the wide universe of individuals attending the symposium would develop unified statements on arts education for the public, the corporate world, boards of education, and artists. These statements should emphasize the critical role of the arts in our culture, he said, stressing that the reform of arts education should follow the protocols established in reading, writing, math, and science.

Sue Heath (Utah Arts Council) stated that she had come to Interlochen for further clarification in the areas noted by Pioli and to share ideas with those of "like mind." Her wish was that, after the three days, symposium participants would be able to win other converts to the arts across the country.

As a superintendent of schools, Donald Bemis (Utica Community Schools, Michigan) emphasized the tremendous resistance the arts must overcome in order to gain an equal place in the curriculum. He agreed that the arts are critical to the future health of our culture, and he was pleased that the discussions planned for the symposium would focus on the quality of arts education.

Shirley Trusty Corey (New Orleans School System) described her school system as the twenty-fifth largest in the country, with an 86-percent minority enrollment. She stressed the urgency of establishing standards by which educators can measure the effectiveness of arts education. Having been involved in the field for a number of years, Corey observed, "Sometimes, it's the same old issues, but it's a new day."

Gary Goree (Tulsa, Oklahoma, Public Schools) noted that Oklahoma, despite economic crises, has given due priority to arts education. It was his hope that the symposium could identify ways in which various groups could work together to make the arts available to all the nation's children.

Pam Sharp (San Francisco Educational Fund)

expressed her wish that the participants would develop a sense of
unity in the field. She hoped that some of the discussions would
focus on what arts providers have to offer in strengthening the
arts curriculum.

John McLaughlin closed the session by reviewing the next day's schedule and explaining
the structure of the breakout sessions. He reiter-
ated the planners' intention that the design of
the symposium give participants, as experts in
the field, the opportunity to react to the papers
and develop recommendations for the improvement of arts education.

The group then adjourned to the recital hall where they were
treated to an hour-long showcase by Interlochen students which
included instrumental solos and ensemble work, slides of student
artwork, dance pieces, theater scenes, and choral singing and
demonstrated how a quality education in the arts can forge the
way for America's cultural future.

The day concluded, participants returned to their rooms; many
had not yet unpacked. Most were fatigued from their journeys and
the evening's activities, but all were excited about the next three
days.

Friday morning brought the first major crisis when the content
committee learned that Richard Sinatra's plane had been delayed
and would not arrive until afternoon. The schedule was hurriedly
rearranged, with Kathryn Martin and Jerrold Ross's session moved
up to first, to be followed by Robert Glidden and Thomas Shannon.

Martin and Ross began their session on "Developing Professionals for Arts Education" with a plea to participants to examine
where and how change might take place. They looked first at the
need for effective preservice education. Then, turning to the topic
of staff development for teachers already in the schools, they
stressed the need for retraining teachers in the delivery of quality
arts education. They also noted deficiencies in the training of

generalist teachers, who often have major responsibilities for teaching the arts in elementary schools. In closing, they asked participants to consider the role of community arts agencies in the in-service education process.

Following the first breakout session, the participants reconvened for the next full session, "Improvement of Arts Education: Planning Over the Long Term." The authors of this paper, Robert Glidden and Thomas Shannon, began their presentation by emphasizing that many good things were happening in arts education but that there was still room for improvement. Glidden urged his audience to consider what they could do to change society's value system so that the arts would be valued more highly. He stressed the need for articulate, visionary leaders capable of presenting persuasive arguments for the arts in the school setting. Shannon called for a better understanding of the political process, of how it relates to the kind of improvements the field is striving  for. He observed that arts education leaders, unlike Alice in Wonderland, must not seek merely to go "someplace" but must decide exactly where that place is and what the best strategies are for getting there. In developing those strategies, the arts should look to the curricular successes of athletics, math, and the sciences.

The afternoon session, led by Richard Sinatra and co-author Paul Lehman, focused on their paper, "Arts Curricula in the Schools: Their Role, Content and Purpose." Sinatra recounted his experiences in Naples when he was studying classical guitar. After realizing that he would never become a performing artist, he decided that his abilities were best suited to curriculum. Comparing the arts curriculum to other areas of curricular reform, Sinatra warned arts educators not to teach parts of the arts in isolation from the whole, not to fragment the curriculum. He strongly advised careful consideration of the evaluation process and conscientious efforts to make certain that thinking skills of the highest level were being taught and evaluated. He also stressed that arts leaders must be involved in the curriculum planning process. In short, he concluded, the arts should learn from the other disciplines and avoid some of their mistakes in the process of curricular reform.

Lehman took a different approach and remonstrated the group not to speak as if there were no programs, no curriculum, no informed teachers, but rather to support existing programs—a role he deemed particularly appropriate for arts advocates. Among the problems most in need of the arts community's attention, Lehman pointed to the failure of the arts to reach all students; the lack of adequate support for teachers; the insufficient amount of time accorded the arts in the curriculum; and the extremely low priority given to theater and dance in the schools, as compared to music and the visual arts.

Following the afternoon meeting, the recorders from each of the breakout sessions spent an hour compiling summary recommendations for the day's topics. At 4:30, the full symposium reconvened to hear the results. The presenters felt they had not had enough time to fully discuss the many topics that had come before the ten breakout groups, and they warned that their presentations would be little more than a series of incomplete and unfocused recommendations and thoughts.

It was also clear that each of the groups had approached discussion of the papers differently. Each of the first three papers had addressed some of the most volatile issues of arts education—what curriculum should be taught, who should teach it, and how teachers should be trained. On these topics many participants had strong and very conflicting points of view. With some groups, one point raised about a paper encompassed their entire discussion. With others, the divergent opinions of arts providers vs academics or arts educators deflected the discussion to side issues. The first day of small group interaction revealed many of the difficulties involved in reaching consensus in such a diverse field as arts education.

The presentations were followed by a question-and-answer

period with the authors of the day's papers. It began quietly, but within minutes a heated exchange erupted between the steering committee and the participants. Among the concerns raised were the following:

- The need for leadership
- The need for agreement on fundamentals and on some basic statements
- Problems resulting from the wide range of backgrounds of the participants
- Lack of substantive issues
- Expecting too much too soon
- The role of "The Philadelphia Resolution" and the "Concepts" documents in relationship to the expected recommendations from the symposium
- Terminology
- Recognition of the arts education movement
- The desire to modify the second day's agenda

This frustration and explosiveness embodied the central problems of arts education. Here was a field of innumerable organizations and individuals either working directly in schools or providing services to schools which had had little communciation with one another over the past decade. The arts community had developed a vocabulary of its own, one little understood by educators; on the other hand, educators used terminology standard to that field. Each world viewed the other as suspect due to a lack of basic understanding of how the other functioned. At this point in the symposium, eight hours had not been enough to heal wounds that had developed over the years or to bridge the wide gulf of understanding that permeated the teaching of the arts. It remained to be seen if, in the second day, participants could put aside their individual differences and find common ground to discuss the practical strategies needed for the long-term improvement of arts education.

When the plenary session concluded, the content committee met to discuss what had happened and to rethink the second day. In the end, they elected to maintain the agenda as planned, with one major change: each of the ten groups would be asked to come up with three recommendations reflecting all of the discussions held over the two days. These recommendations would serve as the focus of the second plenary session.

 Saturday morning, everyone awoke to a beautiful, invigorating fall day. The first presentation, "Partnerships in Arts Education: Teachers, Artists and Scholars," was led by Charles Dorn and Lonna Jones, with Jones discussing the history of partnerships over a 20-year period. Some individuals had been left out of partnerships, she stated, and it was time to reconsider who the partners should be. She also pointed out that the current emphasis on the whole child and the whole curriculum should be foremost in the minds of those involved in the planning process. Dorn asked the group to determine where partnerships would work best. He noted three problem areas in which partnerships might lead to resolutions: school arts curriculum, delivery of instruction, and education of teachers.

For their session—"Partnerships for Arts Education: Organizations, Agencies and Institutions"—Richard Bell and Jonathan Katz departed from the established format and made a joint presentation. They asked that participants use the lists in their paper as checklists, or as a model exercise through which they could examine their commitment to partnerships and discover how to forge new ones. The authors suggested that these partnerships should form the basis for a collective vision of the future of arts education. Participants could continue rechecking the lists in the months to come as they pursued their individual work in arts education.

Lunchtime conversations indicated that participants were much happier with the day's first session than they had been with those of the day before, and it appeared that a consensus was being reached in each group. In opening the last of the six sessions,

"Advocacy and Action: Strategies for Strengthening Arts Education," Stephen Kaagan strongly urged the participants to acquaint
themselves with the process of change in the local setting. The
arts must have a much stronger repertoire of political and advocacy strategies, he insisted. Next, he discussed the relationship between state departments of education and local school systems
and how arts educators must understand this relationship if they
are to effect significant changes in what happens in school classrooms. Co-author Sarah Chapman stressed the need for local coa-
litions of cultural institutions and higher education facilities to
work effectively with school systems.

At the second plenary session, sets of recommendations were
presented by representatives from each of the ten groups. One
group, unable to confine themselves to the requested three recommendations, had come up with five. An intense sense of pride and
accomplishment was shared by the participants, all of whom felt
that the 32 statements presented by the ten groups included policy
and program recommendations that could indeed lead the field
into a new era.

That night, a small group of sympo-
sium members, including Charles Fowler,
Sarah Chapman, Stephen Kaagan, and
John Mahlmann, compiled the 32 recommendations into a three-page resolution for
presentation at the final brunch.

Next day, the resolution was read to the full assembly by
Charles Fowler. After a brief presentation and acknowledgments
by John Mahlmann and Milton Rhodes, the participants were
given an opportunity to make additional suggestions. With a few
reservations, everyone expressed their satisfaction with the version
of the resolution that appears later in this book.

The three days in the woods had come to an end, and consensus had been reached on many issues. Differences of opinion and
issues still remain to be addressed, and the task ahead is not an
easy one. The national groups, representing both the arts and the

education communities, have begun to talk with each other, to understand each other, and to plan for the future. These discussions, agreements and mutual understandings need to continue to evolve over the next few years. More importantly, what happened over the course of the three days spent in Michigan in November, 1987, must be repeated in local communities across America. In each community, where a school system exists along with arts advocates, artists and cultural institutions, discussions must be initiated about how all of these co-equal partners can directly affect what children learn in the arts. The national groups must work in concert with each other and through their individual networks to facilitate these local level discussions. Otherwise, the three days in the woods will have been for naught. Those in arts education—all those involved in educating children in the arts—must now move forward and continue to listen to each other and to plan together. Only this can move our nation toward a new era in arts education.

2
The Papers

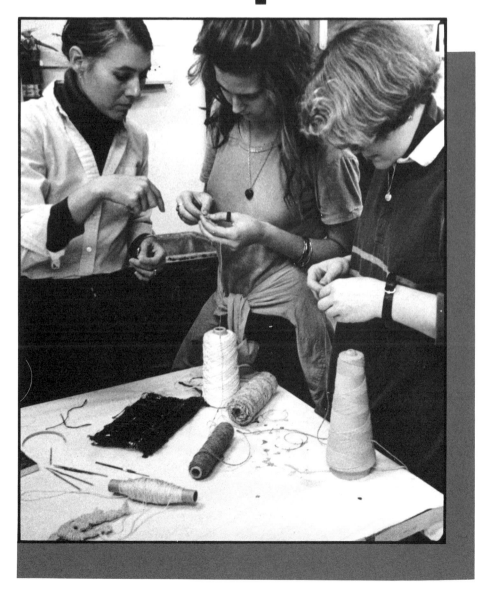

Kathryn A. Martin and Jerrold Ross

DEVELOPING PROFESSIONALS FOR ARTS EDUCATION

T he quality of arts education in U.S. schools depends upon the training and qualifications of arts teachers. What are the challenges, then, to developing successful professional arts educators.

IDENTIFYING PROFESSIONALS IN ARTS EDUCATION

The term "professional" as applied to arts teachers has multiple meanings, as several kinds of "professionals" are teaching the arts in U.S. elementary and secondary schools—the professional arts educator, the professional teacher and the professional artist. In a strict sense, the term really applies only to those who have been prepared for a career as a music educator or art educator (and in some localities dance educator or drama and theater educator) at an institution of higher education and who have been approved for certification. From the middle of the nineteenth century, when music education in the United States began in Boston under Lowell Mason, until today, the notion has been almost universally accepted that, in the formal school system, the arts should be taught primarily by trained and certified teachers from the discipline of either art or music. Most of today's art and music teachers have been graduated from professional teacher preparation programs and are officially certified by standards established by state education departments, the states having the authority to certify teaching professionals.

The means by which professional arts educators are made available to the schools vary from one school district to another. Most certified music and art teachers are employed to teach at the secondary level, as the graduation requirements for high school students in many states include some instruction in one or both of these subjects.[1] Although elementary schools are much less likely than secondary schools to employ art or music teachers, many school districts do so—usually those in more affluent communities. Some school districts arrange for what is considered ideal—an elementary-school classroom teacher working with an arts specialist (whose contact with students is seldom more than once a week).

Most elementary school teachers have had at least one course in music or art education as part of their basic training. The rationale is that the teacher of kindergarten through sixth grade, as a "generalist," should include working with art and music as part of regular classroom responsibilities in the overall curriculum. However, the majority of such teachers, having had little experience in the arts themselves, are not completely comfortable in the arts, and the degree of their concern for arts education in the classroom thus often reflects their individual interest and enthusiasm for the field.

There are also significant differences from district to district in the availability of the various arts disciplines in schools. Although considered ideal for communities that can afford to do so, the employment of dance and theater educators is rare because only a minority of states have made provision for certifying dance and theater teachers. In some schools dance is taught by regular school personnel—usually physical education teachers, who are certified in that field and have had little training in dance. Theater is usually taught by certified English teachers, who may have a personal interest in fostering dramatics.

Teachers who have some expertise in any of the arts may be employed in other ways. Large school districts with a surplus of tenured (permanently employed) teachers have often assigned elementary-school classroom teachers or, in the secondary schools, teachers of certain other disciplines to teach one of the arts. This practice is not uncommon in the more academic disciplines as well. Frequently, however, these teachers are just one step ahead of the students.

Another type of professional arts educator is the professional artist. As far back as the Great Depression, professional artists were employed under the Works Progress Administration (WPA) to play a role in the schools. During the terms of Presidents Kennedy, Johnson and Nixon, substantial funds were made available for school districts to employ practicing artists as "artists-in-residence" in both elementary and secondary schools.

Thus the term "professional" as applied to classroom teachers or teachers trained in disciplines other than the arts refers only to their principal occupation—that of teaching—but not to their training as artists or teachers of an art. Professional artists in school residency programs are also recognized as "professionals," but again, not because of their training as professional arts educators but rather because of their performances, exhibitions and critical reviews and because their principal source of income derives from such creative activities. Thus those working as "professionals" in arts education can have quite different training and experience.

TRAINING ARTS TEACHERS

The training of arts teachers has two major components which, though seldom designed to complement and support each other, are often confused: preservice and inservice training.

Theoretically, preservice training is the part of teacher education that takes place in the baccalaureate years of college, whereas inservice programs are generally those courses or activities required by a school district, usually in the first years of teaching. For instance, a person with a baccalaureate degree in music education might be hired to teach K-6 music education in a school district. The district might then require that the teacher take three units of inservice training during the first five years of teaching. The same teacher might also be required to obtain a master's degree either in education or in music before acquiring lifetime certification.

School districts often provide opportunities for receiving a "unit" of inservice education. For example, several years ago a school district in Indiana, having determined that additional work in creative dramatics would benefit elementary- and middle-school language arts teachers, hired a creative drama specialist to conduct a one-day workshop for one inservice unit in Creative Dramatics for these teachers. In most instances, however, inservice education efforts are not focused on eliminating deficiencies in teachers' skills or knowledge. Most often teachers simply select from a smorgasbord of courses at nearby colleges and universities those that meet their inservice requirements rather than their needs.

Inservice activities are generally scheduled during an orientation period before the academic year begins or in the middle of an academic year. Throughout the 1960s and 1970s, many school districts provided opportunities for inservice training at the end of the school day. However, union contracts often blocked the opportunity for such after-school activities unless the teachers were paid additional salary. The costs to the school districts of providing salary in addition to the costs of the inservice training often made it impossible for them to offer inservice opportunities. This predicament must be addressed.

IDENTIFYING SOURCES
OF CURRICULAR CONTROL

Teacher education currently takes place in a variety of four-year colleges and universities. The curricula vary from state to state, depending upon the requirements of the state education agency, as well as other influences discussed below.The state usually requires a number of pedagogical, philosophical and historical courses related to the general field of education. Although the right to set educational standards is the states' prerogative, additional agencies and organizations have entered the field over many decades, among them professional accrediting groups representing the interests of the disciplines. For example, the National Association of Schools of Music, National Association of Schools of Art and Design, National Association of Schools of Theatre and National Association of Schools of Dance—all provide academic institutions with frameworks for determining teacher-certification requirements in each of the arts.

Other voluntary associations to which colleges and universities belong, including such important organizations as regional accrediting groups, also influence curricula. Therefore it is not unusual for a university program designed, for example, to prepare teachers for early childhood education to be accredited first by the respective state education agency, then by the National Council on Accreditation of Teacher Education (NCATE) and—because of discrete philosophies and practices in early childhood education—then by yet another voluntary group (for example, the Montessori Society).

Teacher education thus reflects the fragmentation of our society into groups and splinter groups, each designed to protect the special interests of a particular field or body of practitioners. The requirements of the state education department are mandatory. However, membership in all the rest is voluntary, though the pressure to be accredited by these other groups is strong, particularly at the larger institutions of higher education. At a recent Wingspread meeting of Deans of Colleges of Education, Colleges of the Arts and Sciences, and Graduate Schools, the education deans were hard-pressed to explain the array of accrediting groups to which many arts education programs have chosen to respond.

Less obvious, but still influential in the development of educational programs and projects for training art, music, dance or theater teachers, were the private funding sources and, between the late 1950s and mid-1970s, federal government agencies.

Among the private sources, foundations and corporations effected changes in arts education through their selection of grant recipients (although these grants were often the result of extensive collaboration with professional leaders, including officers in state and national arts education groups). The influence of the private sector was further strengthened by its close collaborations with public funding sources, and by the close relationships among the individuals in charge of distributing funds from either or both sources.

Among the major federal agencies, the National Endowment for the Humanities and the National Endowment for the Arts have also sought to influence the educational process, as did their predecessors. Funds made available through the National Defense Education Act and legislation dealing with children with disabilities or economic disadvantages, or gifted and talented children, were also administered by the U. S. Office of Education or the now defunct Office of Economic Opportunity. Across the country governmental agencies fostered arts education projects deemed "innovative"—projects employing new teaching approaches that could be replicated elsewhere—with administrators and staffs providing strong direction. Educational policies and practices have at times been dominated by the regulations of all these acts and agencies under the auspices of which hundreds of millions of dollars were spent.

Given the array of influences on curricula, the question arises: who *should* determine the content of education for teachers of the arts? Clearly, the practitioners of the discipline currently have the least control: in teacher training generally and in the arts particularly, the practitioners have singularly limited impact on the content. Meanwhile, teacher education programs answer to a variety of accrediting bodies and the state's determination of what courses an individual must have to be "certified," as well as to the advocacy and lobbying efforts of schools and colleges of education.

The issue of control of the curriculum is especially important at this moment in history when states are considering new criteria for certification. For example, Michigan is developing "subject area examinations" given to measure prospective teachers' grasp of subject matter. However, an understanding of the subject matter probably accounts for less than half the requirements for being a successful arts teacher. In addition to subject matter knowledge and understanding, of greatest importance is the individual's ability to apply that knowledge.

The questions concerning testing teachers for subject matter knowledge are many, and the answers are critical to the future of teacher-education programs in the arts. Who will determine the nature and content of these examinations? What role will practitioners and accrediting agencies have in determining the content of the examination? How will applicability of the knowledge and information be tested? To influence the answers to these questions, state arts agencies, arts education organizations and higher education need to form, as quickly as possible, consortia with other organizations interested in arts education.

If interest groups, rather than individuals in higher education and in the classroom, are to determine what should be taught, the problems of teacher education will remain unsolved. This is not to suggest that there are not many outstanding teachers in today's classrooms, but rather to say that they provide quality teaching in the arts almost despite their training rather than because of it. Too often preservice training programs—specifically those courses required for certification outside the area of a major—do little to enhance the individual's teaching ability. The question then arises as to what sort of training would enhance those abilities.

FOSTERING SUCCESSFUL TEACHING THROUGH CURRICULAR REFORM

What are the qualities and characteristics required of a successful teacher? If teachers are truly the architects of enduring quality, supporting the best in each child day after day, what does this require of the individual called "teacher?" Robert Rauschenberg described his experience of knowing Josef Albers as a faculty member at Black Mountain College in 1948:

> He didn't teach you how to "do art." The focus was on the development of your own personal sense of looking. When he taught watercolor, for example, it was about learning the specific properties of watercolor—not about making a good picture. Drawing was about the efficient functioning of line.
>
> Color was about the flexibilities and complex relation- ships colors have to one another. All these things in a sense were about—don't trust your own ideas, because things are more specific than that.
>
> I found his criticism in class so excruciating and devastating that I never asked for private criticism, which you could do there. Years later, though, I'm still learning what he taught me. What he taught had to do with the whole

visual world, and it applies to whatever you're doing, gardening or painting or whatever.[2]

To be remembered as Rauschenberg remembers Albers assists us in drawing some conclusions as to the qualities of a good teacher. The quality of clarity is most obvious. On the other hand, "to be clear," to have clarity in one's presentation requires an in-depth knowledge of subject matter. It requires study of the history and philosophy that have contributed to the subject matter. Perhaps of greatest importance to clarity is a self-confident knowledge of the discipline in which one is teaching. Certainly in the arts, a thorough knowledge of the discipline, of the history and the criticism that have determined quality in the discipline, is essential for the classroom teacher. Knowledge of discipline and a resulting clarity in the presentation of the subject matter results in an individual who is capable of facilitating the creative process, rather than the individual who uses repeated intervention to change the direction of a child's, young person's or adult's work. The teacher who combines knowledge of the discipline with the ability to present the subject matter clearly is capable of facilitating the creative process, in contrast to the individual who uses repeated intervention to change the direction of a student's work. The difference between facilitation and intervention is not significantly different from the concept of negotiation.[3] Negotiation, when pursued correctly, suggests a "win-win" rather than a "win-lose" positioning of ideas. For one to facilitate, the individual can never lose sight of the fact that in the great arena of thinking all ideas are equal, and we all learn from each other whether the facilitator/teacher or a second or third grader. As one facilitates, one is better able to empower, and does not find it necessary to control. And, again, the ability to empower requires self-confidence in one's knowledge of the discipline. We find ourselves most apt to control, rather than empower when we are put on the defensive.

Unfortunately, these characteristics are oftentimes only subconsciously the goals of preservice teacher education. Rather, the preservice teacher education that takes place in our colleges and universities is primarily content, with more emphasis on the content of education courses than on the content of the discipline or major. In fact, in most states a person majors in elementary education, and is not discipline based.

The thrust of the educational process must shift toward much greater emphasis on the content of the discipline. A rather radical position is that of not having any education courses, historical perspectives, etc. until after the student, particularly in the arts, receives the baccalaureate degree. Whether the baccalaureate is in a studio area or in history and criticism, the baccalaureate should be the first requirement for entrance into a master teaching program in the arts.

Higher education must also begin to address the relationship of preservice education to inservice offerings. Rarely do these two types of training complement each other. Greater effort should be made at the time of preservice training to indicate the importance and the nature of inservice courses that will be available to students once they finish their undergraduate education.

Teachers in schools or colleges of fine arts should make better use of the continuing education arms of their universities. There are opportunities for offering updated inservice activities in such fields as new materials, further integration of art history and aesthetics into the arts curriculum, refresher courses in music for elementary and secondary music teachers, and courses in computers and technology in the teaching of music and composition. Work is being done in all these areas in colleges and universities, but the inservice courses provided are often those courses that the faculty want to teach rather than those that would meet specific deficiencies and needs of the classroom teacher or art specialist.

Higher education must begin now to provide leadership in the design of inservice courses, addressing such questions as how inservice education might be better coordinated to meet the needs and deficiencies of teachers, rather than being determined by what professors would prefer teaching; how agencies outside the schools might participate in planning; and how teachers might take part in planning and carrying out inservice work without such activities becoming a financial burden to the school district. One method of providing inservice training that deserves to be explored is having teachers train other teachers, not necessarily those from the same school, but perhaps from within the same system. Teachers with special strengths, such as a music teacher who has taken the time to learn to use a computer in music education, might well provide inservice training for other music teachers. The same is true of the visual arts, drama and dance.

Only when these questions are answered and solutions found to the problems can the nation attain the quality teacher training and inservice education needed to ensure more than a mediocre school system.

PROPOSING NEW TEACHING STANDARDS

Over the past five years many voices have expressed the need for
reform of education, with emphasis on changing how professionals are prepared to teach. Chief among the books and national
studies is the report of the Carnegie Commission. The Carnegie
Task Force on Teaching as a Profession is proposing a National
Board for Professional Teaching Standards, which would establish
minimum standards for the certification of teachers. A certificate
issued by this group, it is argued, would be beneficial to the profession, indicating by means of "an unambiguous statement that
its holder is a highly qualified teacher."[4] The Carnegie group advocates that states add their own requirements to whatever standards are adopted or that they use those of the National Board
exclusively. The implications for the certification of art, music (or
dance and theater) educators remain to be seen.

Closely allied to this movement is a new organization called
the Holmes Group, a consortium of approximately one hundred
research universities. It endorses many of the provisions of the
Carnegie report, including the establishment of a National Board,
the use of "lead" or "master" teachers, a specific degree (Master
of Teaching) that lead teachers would have to hold, and continuing education offered by school districts or schools of education.
The Holmes Group also supports a three-tiered system of teacher
licensing, including master teachers.

Neither the Carnegie report nor the Holmes Group addresses
the issue of exactly how these standards will be developed. Nor
do they provide any definition of a teaching professional other than
the certified (or licensed) teacher, except to say that teachers, themselves, should have the largest role in determining such standards.

However, to capitalize on the "reform" movements, this
might be the time for arts education groups to insist on increasing
the numbers of art, music, dance or theater teachers to support
the notion of quality promulgated by Holmes and Carnegie, and to
ensure that arts educators be just as eligible as others for the up-
ward professional mobility provided for in the recommendations
for teacher licensing.

MEETING FUTURE NEEDS

At present, there is a need to prepare a minimum of 13,000 teachers of arts, music, dance and theater over the next five years.[5] In

urban areas, the need for trained arts teachers will be acute. There, the departure of young teachers from the profession because of low salaries and poor working conditions is a major concern across the nation. The need may never really be met. The attraction of teaching for performers and visual artists has lessened considerably over the past decade, and boards of education have not moved quickly enough (nor do they appear likely to do so) to create salaries even somewhat competitive with business and industry. Bright young artistic people, who might otherwise have considered education as a profession, are easily attracted to jobs in the arts business, arts technology, or administration, and are continuing to make their way as free-lance creators—as many of their predecessors have always done.

Nevertheless, the profession of arts education must continue to try to recruit these future teachers and artists to work in the schools; indeed, it must redouble its efforts to attract and maintain teachers in the classrooms. As governmental priorities have changed during the Reagan years, resources external to the schools, however beneficial, have received greatly diminished support. The once-powerful artist-in-residence program of the National Endowment for the Arts has faltered, and only a few groups, such as Affiliate Artists and Young Audiences, have demonstrated much staying power.

In the foundation and corporate world, support for arts education has foundered. One might welcome the renewed interest and intervention in arts education of such powerful agencies as the John D. Rockefeller III Fund, the Rockefeller Foundation, the Ford Foundation, Mobil, Exxon and other private funding grants.

In the federal apparatus, too, arts education has "fallen between the cracks" of the National Endowment for the Arts and the National Endowment for the Humanities, the former dedicated to performance and creation, and the latter, to scholarly research and programs. Whereas in the old Department of Education (later, the Department of Health, Education and Welfare) a branch was devoted to arts education, nowhere does that arm now exist. No one in Washington speaks for arts education anymore. However, the Arts Endowment and the Department of Education have just announced the joint funding of an arts education research center, marking the culmination of an aim long held by both agencies—that arts education should be the subject of joint action.

EXPLORING THE NEXT STEPS

Various steps have been suggested to improve teacher training and certification as well as to expand employment opportunities for future arts educators. The following are among them:

1. Setting goals, locality by locality, for the recruitment of arts teachers;

2. Creating certification for dance and theater teachers in the schools, paralleling certification for art and music teachers;

3. Creating more jobs for arts educators, with better salaries and working conditions;

4. Influencing and educating members of local and state boards of education, helping them to understand these problems;

5. Working with national educational organizations (National Education Association, American Federation of Teachers) and others to raise salaries and improve working conditions;

6. Influencing foundations and corporations to increase support for arts education.

7. Helping to reestablish arts education as a priority in the Office of Education.

8. Effecting closer relationships between federal agencies (the Office of Education and the Arts and Humanities Endowments) on behalf of arts education;

9. Revising arts education curricula in keeping with recent reform efforts;

10. Establishing collaborations between artists, arts educators and classroom teachers to help revitalize education curricula in the arts.

Education is the foundation of our future and the arts are often perceived as the key to our environment. The following quotation from Pablo Casals suggests the urgency of finding solutions:

> Each second we live in a new and unique moment of the universe. And what do we teach our children in school? We teach them that two and two make four and that Paris is the capital of France. When will we also teach them what they are? We should say to each of them: Do you know what you are? You are a marvel. You are unique. In all the world there is no other child exactly like

you. And look at your body . . . what a marvel it is! Your legs, your arms, your cunning fingers, the way you move!! You may become a Shakespeare, a Michelangelo, a Beethoven. You have the capacity for anything. Yes, you are a marvel. And when you grow up, can you then harm another who is, like you, a marvel?[6]

Notes

1. The numbers of students enrolled in some form of arts courses in secondary schools (no figures are available for the elementary level) in the school year 1981/82 were 2,733,000 in music (22 percent of the secondary school-age population); 2,143,000 in art (18 percent); 236,000 (1 percent) in areas defined as acting/play production; and 30,000 (0.3 percent) in dance, rhythm.

   In the 1983/84 school year, elementary and secondary schools employed approximately 79,100 full-time-equivalent teachers of music and 50,700 teachers of art. U. S. Office of Education (Center for Educational Statistics), *Teachers in Elementary and Secondary Schools* (Washington, D.C.: March 1987).

2. Calvin Tomkins, *Off The Wall* (New York: Penguin Books, 1980), 32.

3. Roger Fisher and William Ury, *Getting to Yes* (New York: Penguin Books, 1983).

4. Carnegie Forum on Education and the Economy. *A Nation Prepared: Teachers for the 21st Century* (New York: The Carnegie Corporation, 1986).

5. Although no statistics are available on the ages of arts teachers, if the age groups among them parallel those among the general teacher population, approximately 10,500 arts teachers will probably be retiring over the next five years, and another 2,500 will leave the profession after their first few years of service.

6. Gerald L. Knieter and Jane Stallings, eds., *The Teaching Process and Arts and Aesthetics* (St. Louis: Cemrel, 1979), 1.

Bibliography

Carnegie Forum on Education and the Economy. *A Nation Prepared: Teachers for the 21st Century*. New York: The Carnegie Corporation, 1986.

Fisher, Roger and William Ury. *Getting to Yes*. New York: Penguin Books, 1983.

Fiske, Edward B. "Redesigning the American Teacher," *New York Times*, April 12, 1987, Section 12, p. 18.

Getty Trust. *Beyond Creating: The Place for Art in America's Schools*. Los Angeles: Getty Center for Education in the Arts, 1985.

Holmes Group. *Tomorrow's Teachers*. East Lansing, Michigan: The Holmes Group, 1986.

Knieter, Gerard L. and Jane Stallings, Editors. *The Teaching Process and Arts and Aesthetics*, p. 1, St. Louis: Cemrel, 1979.

Ross, Jerrold. "Who Shall Teach the Arts," *Design for Arts in Education*, vol. 87, no. 6 July-August 1986:9-12. Washington, D.C.

Shaker, Paul and Walter Ullrich. "Reconceptualizing the Debate Over the General Education of Teacher," *Teacher Education*, vol. XXXVIII, no. 1 January-February 1987:11-15. Washington, D.C.

Tomkins, Calvin. *Off The Wall*. New York:Penguin Books, 1980.

U.S. Office of Education (Center for Educational Statistics), *Teachers in Elementary and Secondary Schools*. Washington, D.C.: March, 1987.

Robert Glidden and Thomas Shannon

PLANNING LONG-TERM IMPROVEMENTS IN ARTS EDUCATION

T here can be little question that arts education in the United States needs improvement and that the present time is propitious. The current interest in educational improvement at all levels, brought about by a spate of national reports and critiques on education, affords an opportunity for focusing attention on the arts as an important component in the comprehensive education of all Americans.

BUILDING ON STRENGTHS

Planning for improvement should build on the strengths of arts education. A number of those strengths were cited in a recent briefing paper on K-12 arts education in the United States issued by eight of the most prominent organizations in the field. The paper noted (1) the devotion of individual teachers to developing skills and knowledge of the arts disciplines in others; (2) the existence of a framework for the delivery of curriculum-based arts education through public schools, private schools, community arts schools, private teachers and a variety of other means; (3) the strong tradition of school-based arts education programs in many U. S. communities; (4) a fundamentally sound structure for teacher preparation in higher education; and (5) a committed and creative industry related to, and interested in, K-12 arts education.[1]

These strengths—the result of many years of dedicated work by thousands of educators and artists—are to be applauded. However, a more critical diagnosis of the present situation is necessary if improvement is to be forthcoming. The briefing paper, after noting those strengths, included the caveat that ''the enumeration of these basic strengths should not be construed as denying that fundamental problems exist. Each of the areas we have delineated has numerous examples of dysfunction and even dissolution.''[2]

IDENTIFYING THE ISSUES

If Americans are not being educated effectively in the arts, what
are the problems and what are the issues to be confronted? Four
problems seem paramount:

1. Too little time devoted to arts in the school day;

2. The public's lack of recognition of the value of the arts in
   people's lives and of the importance of developing basic
   artistic skills and concepts at an early age;

3. Insufficient rigor and expectation; and

4. A lack of energetic and visionary leadership on the part of
   both arts educators and school administrators, which has
   resulted in a lack of focus on the significance of arts education by local school board policy makers;

The lack of time in the school day is undoubtedly the greatest
obstacle to effective arts education for all youth. No precise data
fully reveal how much time is devoted to education in the arts in
U. S. schools, but observations indicate that most elementary-
school students probably receive less than one hour a week, depending to some extent on what school activities are included as
"artistic." Secondary-school students certainly average far less
than that. In contrast, a recent study of Japanese education by the
U. S. Department of Education reveals that Japanese students are
required to study music for 90 minutes a week and art and handi-
craft for 90 minutes a week through the eighth grade; 45 minutes
of music and 45 minutes of fine arts a week in the ninth grade;
and music or calligraphy through grade 12, the amount depending
upon the year and focus of study.[3]

It would seem that Americans do not have high expectations
of their children in the arts, at least through formal schooling. For
example, arts achievement is not typically included in the standardized testing of general educational achievement at any level.
The low expectation of achievement may result from the lack of
time provided to arts education, or the opposite may be true.
Whatever the case, a substantive, sequential curriculum is impossible to pursue if only a few minutes each week are scheduled for
arts disciplines. Teachers cannot base a lesson plan on what was
learned during the previous class when those sessions are only 20
or 30 minutes long and scheduled a full week apart. They cannot
expect their students to accomplish much under those circumstances. The consequence is a kind of arts education too often
based upon passive experience rather than active involvement

with the arts. Music or art class becomes "play time" in the minds of students rather than a class in which they will be held accountable for specific achievements. All this occurs often through no fault of the teacher, who can do little more than give a best effort during the time available.

Too little time and low expectation—both result from a lack of recognition among parents and school officials that the arts play an important part in our lives. Perhaps most people in our society do not take seriously their own capacity for artistic expression. They may marvel at the technique of a virtuoso violinist or ballerina but give little thought to how important artistic expression is to their own happiness in everyday life. Americans have subscribed too much to the belief that artistic talent and sensibility belong exclusively in the province of intuition: "You either have it or you don't." Such a belief counters arguments in favor of arts education for all youngsters because it denies that the vast majority of people *can* learn to be responsive to, sensitive to, and even expressive with, the arts. Artists and advocates who are interested in developing consumers of the arts would do well to consider that individuals who learn to be artistically expressive themselves will also be more responsive to artistic presentations than those who do not learn to be artistically expressive.

If the American public does not value the arts highly enough, educators must share at least some of the responsibility. Too often perhaps it has been assumed that leadership on such issues as the arts in education would or should come from a higher level—from federal or state authorities, councils or committees. However, as Thomas P. "Tip" O'Neill, Jr., former long-time Speaker of the U. S. House of Representatives, was known to remark, "All politics is local!" That point is as applicable to advocacy for arts education as to any other advocacy. The convincing arguments must be made at the local level to those who determine local school policy.

Several recent initiatives show promise of new resolve, at least among artists and arts educators, to improve arts education in the United States. The K-12 briefing paper previously mentioned is one such effort. It is comprehensive, informative and thought-provoking. The Getty Center for Education in the Arts program for the visual arts is controversial because of its philosophy, but Getty is one of the few large foundations now devoting major resources to the arts, and in this case the program is in arts *education*. The recently formed Foundation for the Advancement of Education in Music (FAEM) is a cooperative effort between educators and segments of the music industry to influence American perception about the importance of music study. Although established too recently for results to be observable, FAEM is the type of effort that should be undertaken in each of the arts disciplines. The National Endowment for the Arts has overhauled its arts education policy within the past two years in what may be regarded as its first significant effort to improve arts education nationwide. The Arts Endowment is also conducting a study on arts education for the Congress. The symposium for which this paper is written is one more indication of the beginning of a new thrust in favor of arts education in the United States.

Improving arts education in the United States is, over the long term, more a political issue than an educational one. The most serious problem is not a lack of knowledge about how to teach the arts but a reluctance to give the time and attention to doing so in a systematic fashion. It is possible that the wrong issue has been addressed under the assumption that the fundamental problem—lack of time—could not be resolved. Arts educators must develop appropriate arguments for their case based on a defensible rationale, and they must find ways to articulate those arguments where they will be heard and to the people who make decisions about education.

ARTICULATING THE RATIONALE
FOR ARTS EDUCATION

One rationale for arts education can be derived from the research of psychologist Howard Gardner and his colleagues. Professor Gardner's Project on Human Potential first draws an educator's attention by its very title: Project on *Human Potential*.[4] It would seem a laudable and appropriate goal of U. S. schools to develop each person to his or her fullest potential. If that were a fundamental aim, the first task would be to identify those areas of potential for each individual. Gardner's theory, based upon research in psychology, biology and findings concerning knowledge in different cultures, is that human intellectual competence rests on several "relatively autonomous" areas: linguistic, musical, logical-mathematical, spatial, bodily-kinesthetic and personal intelligence. Study in the arts, as any arts educator would be quick to point out, can relate directly to all those areas of intellectual competence, except perhaps logical-mathematical.

Historically, formal schooling in U. S. society has given heavy weight to linguistic and logical-mathematical intelligences (readin', writin', and 'rithmetic) but relatively slight attention to all others, as they have not been considered "academic." One answer to the question "Why should we learn to experience the arts?" would certainly be that if we do not we are failing to develop important areas of our human potential.

Unfortunately, the arts have too often been sold on the basis of snob appeal, resulting in an image of elitism, both economic and intellectual. Neither is the case, of course. What is true about the arts is that they are unique in their means of expression. They have their own languages and their own messages. It is important to recognize that artistic understanding is not verbally based. That is partly why arts experiences are so special—they often defy verbal definition. They can be emotional or intellectual, realistic or abstract; they may help people to arrive at new thoughts, notions, understandings that they would never have reached otherwise. They help people to imagine in one instance and to define or describe in another. But it is not necessary to *verbalize* the feelings or understanding for those feelings or understanding to be valid and important. The arts belong to the world of ideas, but to a world of nonverbal ideas. This is a difficult point to convey, perhaps especially to educators, who can be so overly concerned about test scores.

STRENGTHENING COLLABORATION

To articulate any argument for improved arts education, it will be important for segments of the arts education community to unite, to develop common purposes and strategies. It is not typical for artists and arts educators to enjoy political pursuits. They see their time as better spent in making or teaching art; which is, of course, what they enjoy doing. Furthermore, politics requires more compromise than is easily accommodated by the individuality of artists. However, good communication and a sense of togetherness in the arts and arts education communities, both within and among groups, will facilitate the progress in arts education that everyone in those communities desires. Political togetherness is not to be confused with togetherness in the classroom, however, where each art has its own fundamentals, its own educational basics. An educational collaboration that emphasizes a combined arts approach to the exclusion of basic learning in each of the arts disciplines could result in the development of a cadre of advanced dilettantes who are prepared for cocktail conversation but not for understanding the symphony or the painting.

It will be up to arts education professionals in the schools to provide the leadership, the energy and the impetus to move arts education to the place on the public agenda that it deserves. This will require hard work, dedication and tenacity in the teachers' home communities. Arts educators must be prepared to match the missionary zeal of those who have a more narrow vision of what constitutes "basic education" in the elementary and secondary schools. As leaders, they must establish clear goals, they must develop plans or strategies to achieve those goals, they must persuade others of the validity of those goals and they must exert the energy to press for acceptance of their goals through patient and persistent advocacy.

To these ends, professional arts education organizations can perform important and constructive services for their members and for arts education in general. They can help formulate goals, identify exemplary programs and help design strategies for the local level. Perhaps most important, professional associations can work cooperatively at national and state levels to engage school administrators and school board members, perhaps through their professional associations, in discussions about the importance of the arts in education. More than 15,000 school districts across the United States are served by some 95,000 school board members, each of whom responds to the particular needs of his or her local community. The arguments must be carried to those school board members, both by association contacts at state and national levels and by individuals at the local level. For that reason the diligent efforts of both individual arts educators and professional arts education associations are important.

EXAMINING THE CURRICULUM

Although the main strategy for improvement must be in the political arena, particularly in the local community, the content and emphasis of arts education are, of course, educational and not political issues. The reason more time for study in the schools is so critical is that the focus should be on developing fundamental skills and ideas in each individual. Such development requires instruction on a regular basis: it requires a sequential curriculum— one in which each lesson builds upon previous ones; and it requires a rigor, at least to the point of providing stated expectations and requiring accountability for what is learned.

Many questions about content remain, however. Should the emphasis be on learning the process of art—"how it works"—or should the emphasis be on the products of art? How much attention should be given to masterworks and how much effort should be made to influence taste? How important is the distinction between art and entertainment? How much time should students spend "doing" art and how much analyzing art? Those are not questions upon which the entire arts education community need agree in order for progress to be made, but they are questions that signal the need for lively discussions in which the nation's intelligentsia and the knowledgeable public as well as artists should participate.

ADDRESSING DEMOGRAPHIC CHANGES

The future of arts education in American schools must be planned with full cognizance of the changing demographics in the nation. That the growth of minority populations, particularly of blacks and Hispanics, far exceeds that of the white population in the United States is well documented. It is also a fact that those populations are not proportionately involved in arts activities in secondary schools, where such activities are often elective. Although it would be inappropriate to charge that arts educators and school officials have intentionally neglected minority populations, the long-term future of the arts in education is dim unless blacks and Hispanics are induced to participate. One means of accomplishing this is to make sure that all children have the same opportunity, which means basic education in the fundamental skills and knowledge of the arts for *all* elementary school youngsters. Careful study needs to be made to determine whether the present lack of participation is attributable to socioeconomic factors or to cultural differences. Can blacks and Hispanics not afford to be involved at the high school level, either because of the cost of equipment and supplies or because it may be perceived that private study is necessary? Or do they not want to take part in activities they regard as being of a culture not their own? What melding of cultures in the curriculum might attract minority students, and what strategies might be employed to convince minority students and their parents that knowledge of the best of Western civilization will be important in their lives? Further, what strategies or incentives might be developed to attract more blacks and Hispanics to the arts teaching professions? One possible solution to the problem of minority participation in school arts activities would be more role models among the faculty.

ADAPTING NEW TECHNOLOGIES

One other challenge that arts educators face in the immediate future is the application of new technology. The capabilities of microcomputers and synthesizers afford exciting new possibilities for teaching creativity in the arts, but at present many students are more conversant with these devices than are the teachers themselves. The ability of schools to provide hardware in sufficient quantities for general classes will be a problem for some time, but perhaps a greater challenge is the harnessing of that electronic brain power for teaching artistic creativity.

PERTINENT QUESTIONS

The following questions seem pertinent to discussions that should both accompany and generate planning for long-term improvement in arts education in the United States. For convenience they are divided into two general categories, those that are philosophical and those that are more operational.

PHILOSOPHICAL QUESTIONS

1. Is a national (not federal) policy regarding the arts in education feasible or advisable?
2. How important are the arts in American society? Can they ever be more important without a better system of arts education? Can artists and arts educators influence society to place greater value on the arts?
3. Why do artists and arts educators think education in the arts is so important? Is it because they believe the arts hold real value for people or is their interest simply a vested one? How does this answer relate to the issue of process-versus-product in arts education?
4. Besides intrinsic artistic values, what other values for young people may be found in the arts: retention in school, social values, exploring other dimensions of human potential? Do

those values in themselves provide sufficient justification for arts education programs?

5. In the content of arts curricula, how much emphasis should be placed on connoisseurship, on teaching the "best of Western civilization"? How much attention should be given to arts from other cultures? Can the two emphases be mixed effectively? What attention should be given to popular forms? What principles apply?

6. How important are measurement and accountability to developing a rationale for arts education? Should the arts be included in standardized achievement tests? If they are not included, can the arts ever reach "full parity" with other academic disciplines?

OPERATIONAL QUESTIONS

1. How can arts educators—the professionals in schools, colleges and universities—influence policy about the future of the arts in U. S. education at the state and local levels?

2. Who will teach the arts in elementary schools—specialists or generalists, and in what mix? What is the *best* approach and what is the most *practicable* approach?

3. How can arts educators convince educational decision makers of the intrinsic value of the arts for young people (and for all people)?

4. How can arts educators educate school administrators about the arts? At what point in administrators' professional preparation might educators intercede? Is there any hope or opportunity for an inservice approach?

5. How can arts educators involve parents in basic arts education, at least to the same extent that parents are involved with education in general or with supporting high- school performing groups?

6. How can arts educators enlist the participation of minority populations in arts education? Can arts education help induce parents from minority groups to become more generally involved in schools than they are at present?

7. How can more minority students, particularly the best students, be induced to become teachers of the arts?

8. How can the results of arts education efforts be measured effectively and efficiently? Can total reliance on verbal abilities be avoided in such measurements? What strategies can

be employed to include the arts in standardized achievement tests?

9. How can local arts groups be educated about the needs of
arts teachers in the schools? How can their support be en-
listed in advocating more time and attention to the arts at
the local school district level?

CONCLUSION

Improvement of arts education over the long term will be dependent upon all of the other topics of focus in this symposium. Certainly arts curricula in the schools will be extremely important.
The "togetherness" of teachers, artists and scholars in a united
front will be critical, as will effective partnerships among arts organizations, agencies and institutions. Recruitment and preparation of young people committed to the cause of education in the
arts for all Americans are essential; and, of course, political strategy and advocacy may be as important as any other factor if improvement is to be realized. There are many strengths upon which
to build and many dedicated professionals to carry the torch. Let
us hope that the Interlochen Symposium is the beginning of an effective effort toward improved arts education in the United States.

Notes

1. *K-12 Arts Education in the United States: Present Context, Future Needs; A
Briefing Paper for the Arts Education Community.* (Reston, Virginia: Music Educators National Conference, National Art Education Association, National Dance Association, American Theater Association,
National Association of Schools of Music, National Association of
Schools of Art and Design, National Association of Schools of Theater, National Association of Schools of Dance, 1986), 18.

2. Ibid.

3. Cynthia Hearn Dorfman, ed., *Japanese Education Today* (Washington,
D.C.: U. S. Department of Education, 1987), 28, 34, 43.

4. Howard Gardner, *Frames of Mind: The Theory of Multiple Intelligences*
(New York: Basic Books, Inc., 1983).

Paul Lehman and Richard Sinatra

ASSESSING ARTS CURRICULA IN THE SCHOOLS: THEIR ROLE, CONTENT AND PURPOSE[1]

W hat is the state of the arts in the nation's elementary and secondary schools today? The truth is that no one really knows. Everyone has formed impressions, and everyone can cite a few anecdotes, but the complete picture is extraordinarily complex. Existing practices include not only the superb and the deplorable but also, between those extremes, a range so diverse that any effort to identify an average would be meaningless.

APPRAISING THE STATE OF THE ARTS IN SCHOOLS

We do know that the state of the arts in education is not so gloomy as some people tend to portray it. Music and art are taught in almost every school in the nation. In 1982 music was taught in 93 percent of the nation's public high schools, up from 88 percent in 1973. It was elected by 22 percent of the student population. Art was taught in 90 percent of the high schools, up from 74 percent in 1973, and elected by 24 percent of the students.[2] There are some 79,000 K-12 music teachers and about 50,000 art teachers across the United States. No figures are available for dance or theater. Music is taught regularly to 9 million elementary school children by music specialists. (Music is often cited here as an example because more data are available about music than about the other arts.)

Further, 22 states now have, or will have by 1989, high-school graduation requirements that include the arts.[3] Twenty of those states have added their requirements since 1980. Several other states are actively considering arts requirements.

Even in states without statewide requirements in the arts some school districts have adopted arts requirements of their own. Although Ohio has no state requirement, a consortium of seven major state universities requires a unit in music, art, theater or dance for admission. In Montana a student must have completed one year in the visual or performing arts to qualify for scholarships at the state universities available to the top 5 percent of the graduating high-school seniors.

Thirty-seven states require the teaching of music in elementary school.[4] In South Carolina the legislature requires every school district to hire one music teacher, one art teacher and one physical education teacher for every 800 elementary students. This requirement is the only one in the nation with a quantitative standard. Though the ratio is inadequate, the principle it embodies is admirable and worth fighting for—whatever the quibbles about the actual numbers.

That is the good news. The bad news is that in too many schools the arts are not taught at all or reach only a small fraction of the students. In many districts and states arts programs have not recovered from cutbacks suffered during the recession of the early 1980s. As a result of Proposition 13, California today has only a tiny fraction of the elementary music specialist positions that existed 15 years ago. In Massachusetts, Proposition 2-1/2 has resulted in the elimination of some 24 percent of the music teaching positions that existed previously.

In the major cities music programs have deteriorated severely since the 1960s. The excellent programs in Philadelphia, Chicago, Los Angeles and other cities have been almost entirely lost, though again the picture is uneven. Many medium-sized and smaller cities have experienced few if any losses, and some programs have been expanded. Austin, Texas, for example, has 90 music specialists for 60 elementary schools—one and a half music teachers for every school. Moreover, Austin has had at least one music specialist in every school since the first elementary school opened there in 1873.

What is being taught in the arts? Who decides? There is no simple answer in any field, but the complexity is even greater in the arts. Textbooks play a less important role in the arts than in other fields of study. Except in elementary general music, they have almost no impact, and even there they reflect practice as much as determine it.

Colleges and universities play a major role in determining the arts curriculum by the ways in which they prepare arts teachers. Much of whatever consensus exists within the current jumble of curricular diversity is directly due to the preservice and inservice education programs of colleges and universities.

Professional associations play a more important role in determining the arts curriculum than those of other fields. At state and national levels, they produce the publications that lay the groundwork for curriculum construction, providing implicit guidance in decisions on curriculum and instruction. Most important of all, they provide the forums for debates that continually reshape the curriculum.

The expectations of the public and of school administrators are also important. They determine not only what is taught in the arts but whether the arts are taught at all. Arts teachers are more dependent than other teachers on short-term, superficial public support, and they rely more heavily on the day-to-day backing of their administrators for funds, facilities and favorable treatment in scheduling.

Finally, what is taught in the arts sometimes depends, unfortunately, on the whims and idiosyncrasies of the individual teacher. The diversity that has resulted has historically been a source of weakness, retarding agreement on clearly defined goals based on skills and knowledge that are taken for granted in other subjects.

IDENTIFYING ASSUMPTIONS ABOUT ARTS EDUCATION

This paper is based on six assumptions. The first is that the arts are an essential part of the curriculum and that they should play a major role in the educational program of every young American. This has been the position of every writer and thinker who has made a major contribution to Western educational thought. It is no less true of major contributors to the current debate on educational reform.[5]

The second assumption is that the arts require serious study. They cannot be learned through random or casual experiences any more than mathematics or biology can. They require regular, systematic programs of sequential study leading to clearly specified aims. They require a curriculum. There is, indeed, something to be learned in the arts beyond superficial pleasure, warm feelings and a vague belief in their inherent goodness. There is content to the arts. That content consists of skills and knowledge. The arts are not merely fun and games.

The third assumption is that arts programs should be directed to all students and not only to the talented. Many professionals in the arts got their start in the schools, but preprofessional training is not the reason for having an arts program. The arts belong in the school because of the joy, the enrichment and the fulfillment they can bring to every human being. They are an essential part of the cultural heritage of every American. They are the essence of civilization itself. They are not for an elite. They are for everyone.

The fourth assumption is that there is no such thing as arts education. That is, arts education is not a single entity. The term is simply a useful convenience for referring, collectively, to education in the individual fields of music, art, theater and dance and creative writing. These fields have much in common, but each has its own content, its own language and its own traditions. They must be learned separately. Brief instruction in ''the arts'' can be helpful in pointing out their commonalities, but no comprehensive program of arts education can be built on the misguided notion that the arts represent a single field of study.

The fifth assumption is that, for serious study to occur, time must be provided for the arts in the school day. One excuse often advanced for why some schools fail to provide a solid program in the arts is that there is simply not enough time in the school day for everything important. John Goodlad, whose 1983 study of the K-12 curriculum was one of the most thorough investigations in the history of education, claims that this is not true. There is time. He proposes that, in a typical elementary school week of 23.5 instructional hours, 1.5 hours should be allocated daily to language arts and one hour to mathematics. It is difficult, he maintains, to conceive of children benefiting proportionately from still more time. He further proposes that 2.5 hours each week be devoted to social studies, 2.5 hours to science and 2.5 to some combination of health and physical education. ''We still have 3.5 hours each week for the arts,'' he concludes.[6] At the secondary level, according to Goodlad, up to 18 percent of each student's program should be devoted to literature and languages; up to 18 percent to mathematics and science; up to 15 percent each to social studies, vocational studies and the arts; and up to 10 percent to physical education.[7] This is the program for every student. It includes 15 percent in the arts. The remaining 10 percent, he believes, should be available to students to pursue their individual interests and abilities, which may, of course, include the arts.

The sixth assumption is that responsibility for instruction in the arts lies primarily with specialist teachers. This is the view of nearly all professional arts educators, though everyone recognizes that the work of the specialist can be greatly assisted by classroom teachers who create an atmosphere favorable to the arts and who carry on instruction in the arts between visits by the specialist.

The reason the arts can best be taught by specialists is that these individuals possess the skills and knowledge that are essential for developing those same skills and knowledge in young people. Some classroom teachers have these abilities, of course, but many do not. The classroom teacher's major contribution can be to make the arts a part of the daily life of the students.

At the same time, in some states and some communities it will be impossible to provide specialists soon. Until specialists can be made available, every school district should make the ability to teach the arts a prerequisite for the employment of classroom teachers. Too many districts claim that the classroom teachers in their schools are teaching the arts, but they do not check to see whether the teachers they hire are able to teach the arts, and they do not check later to see whether the arts are actually being taught. The result is an insidious form of consumer fraud.

DELINEATING THE ROLES OF THE ARTS CURRICULUM

Most people in the arts community are aware that the arts have not been valued as a staple in the school curriculum.[8] The case for art instruction as legitimate content has rested simply on the "general recognition that children love to draw and color and the doing has been its own end."[9] Instruction in the arts has not been viewed in the same way as instruction in the knowledge and skills associated with other domains of the curriculum. If the arts are to be considered basic, they have to compete for time and attention in an already crowded curriculum. A teacher colleague attending an information session on a new state-mandated substance-abuse curriculum raised the concern of many: "Where will this curriculum fit? Do we add another period to our current eight periods a day? Our children are already leading fragmented lives. They go from one separate curriculum to the other with no connectedness to their lives in or out of school."

This is the dilemma for a regular and substantive arts curriculum. Where will it fit? Are the arts necessary and relevant to children's lives? Or will they increase fragmentation by adding one more body of knowledge to the student's agenda for the acquisition of content? If it is to achieve legitimacy, arts instruction needs to contribute to education in three essential ways: (1) the arts must have social utility, that is, provide a social benefit; (2) they must entail fundamental and essential intellectual skills; and (3) they must be capable of systematic organization, teaching and testing, fitting a curriculum pattern or program.[10]

A curriculum is generally a written statement of the aims of a particular discipline, with an extensive menu of the means to achieve and evaluate those aims. Curriculum development is intended to systematize an educational plan in a field or discipline, reflecting what the district believes is valuable for its constituents to learn. Value, as expressed by the collective wisdom of the community, is the key that affords accessibility to the curriculum. The purpose of an arts curriculum, then, is to systematize the standards and specify the time allotted for the learning of a specific arts discipline or form of representation.

Any specific arts curriculum, whether for the visual arts, music, dance, drama or creative writing, has several roles, among them the following:

1. To promote among the general public the view that the arts are crucial to literacy and thinking.

2. To promote within general public education the view that, beyond basic literacy, the arts provide a means for the mind to reach creative heights and to solve problems in novel ways. Arts representations, because they foster diverse modes of thinking, give rise to alternative means of approaching and solving problems.

3. To provide all learners across all grade levels with access to the highest levels of thinking and achievement of western culture, providing a cultural continuity with the past.

4. To establish within state and district curriculum offices the view that arts curricula can be systematized and sequenced through the grades.

5. To establish within the general education community the view that standards in arts instruction can be substantive and rigorous.

6. To establish within the general education community the view that learning in the arts can be assessed.

Each of these roles is examined below.

LITERACY AND THINKING

The arts provide a variety of forms of representation, languages that are necessary to understand and express these forms and the sensory experiences that allow the mind to recall and combine images to form new ideas and perspectives for art. E. L. Boyer expresses this notion:

> Art education, then, is basic because it extends our language. It enlarges the store of the images we use. It makes our understanding discriminating and comprehensive. Music, dance and the visual arts are languages that reach all people at their deepest and most essential human level. Thus, aesthetic literacy is as basic as linguistic literacy.[11]

In contrast to this expansive view of literacy, the National Assessment of Education Progress recently advanced the following: "Using printed and written information to function in society, to achieve one's goals, and to develop one's knowledge and potential."[12]

Are not artistic, nonverbal forms of knowing necessary to "achieve one's goals" and "to develop one's knowledge and potential"? Indeed, although two levels of visual literacy exist for most people of the world, the first level of visual literacy is primary to human thinking and language.[13] This is because the eye is an extension of the brain, and it is through the eye that the young experience, sense and re-create their world in actions and language.

A second stage of visual literacy occurs because of humankind's drive to represent meaning in nonverbal, creative, symbolic and artistic ways. Visual literacy as representational communication is composed of the receptive processes of imagining or composing, the expressive processes of producing or creating and the interactive effects of aesthetic engagement and appreciation. The comprehension and expressiveness gained from each form of literacy provide a richness and a fullness to the others which are continually experienced in a lifetime.

PROBLEM SOLVING

Participation in the arts stimulates representational thinking. During representational thought, one aspect of reality takes on another aspect—as happens, for example, when in the hands of a young child a wooden block becomes a train. Representational thought, which is highly nonverbal and imaginative in nature, is the basis of the thinking of analogy, metaphor and symbol substitution. For young children, representational thought can be expressed in many ways, such as gesture and body language, play, modeling, construction tasks, and drawing and coloring. For older learners, the craft and technique of each art form can be expanded to include as many ways as imagination allows the art form to be re-created.

The power of such methods, in which children's production of art leads to another form of expression, may be that "creativity excites creativity."[14] For instance, poetry can stimulate the scientist, and the discoveries of the scientist can mentally stimulate the creative imagination of the poet. It has been argued that the more creative acts a person experiences, whether those of another or the person's own, the richer the person's life.[15] Anything that makes someone more alive is likely to facilitate and produce creative achievement.

The creative act is often energized by imagery or the re-creation of images.[16] Where does imagery come from and how does it propel intellectual and emotional forces to capture the creative act? These ideas and forces originate and are nourished through all the literacies people experience. Each literacy contributes receptive and expressive symbol systems allowing people to turn raw experience into thought-provoking and emotionally energized images. The broad uses of arts education are "grounded in the generic use of the imagination, that is, the power to create and construe images as vehicles of human import."[17]

CULTURAL CONTINUITY

The presence of the arts in many different cultures "is testimony to the fact that humans have always had a need to explore the aesthetic properties of form and to obtain through them satisfactions and insight that cannot be secured elsewhere."[18] Literature, music and art contain the best evidence of the unity and continuity of the human condition, reflected from past to present.[19] Furthermore, as suggested by the College Board, when students become immersed in the works of other cultures and historical periods, they have the opportunity to learn what occurred beyond bare human survival. They see what was pleasing, beautiful, monumental, extraordinary, shabby, pretentious or unjust. "In studying art works that have stood the test of time, students discover the vision of wholeness and the greater worlds created by humanity's most profound imagination."[20]

STRUCTURE AND SEQUENCE

The arts programs in most schools need more structure and sequence. They need clearer statements of expectations at the various grade levels so that administrators and the public know what results to look for. When no clear goals or expectations are evident it is difficult for arts education to be taken seriously. This view contrasts with that of a more laissez-faire policy of arts instruction in which arts activities are undertaken to allow children to participate in content-free, knowledge-free sessions—as "time off" from more intellectually rigorous aspects of the curriculum.

Here the value of a written curriculum can be acknowledged. A written curriculum provides an articulated conceptual framework for arts content accessible both to those with an arts-oriented background and to those without it. It lays the groundwork and specifies the time allotted for arts activities in the school day. It provides a sequence based on the logic of how learners assimilate a particular arts content. As such, the written document legitimates the arts field or discipline because it carries the same logic and rigors of construction as other curriculum guides.

STANDARDS

The most useful and influential standards in arts education are those published by the professional associations, such as *The School Music Program: Description and Standards*[21] of the Music Educators National Conference (MENC) and *Purposes, Principles, and Standards for School Art Programs*[22] of the National Art Education Association (NAEA). The MENC publication provides standards for course offerings and scheduling, staffing, materials and equipment, and facilities for early childhood, the elementary school, the middle school and the high school. It also provides lists of what students should know and be able to do at the end of grades 3, 6, 9 and 12. In addition, it indicates the music experience that should be provided for preschool children. The NAEA publication provides similar information.

According to the MENC document, the purpose of the elementary and secondary music program should be to produce students who (1) are able to make music, alone and with others; (2) are able to improvise and create music; (3) are able to use the vocabulary and notation of music; (4) are able to respond to music aesthetically, intellectually and emotionally; (5) are acquainted with a wide variety of music, including diverse musical styles and genres; (6) understand the role music has played and continues to play in the lives of human beings; (7) are able to make aesthetic judgments based on critical listening and analysis; (8) have developed a commitment to music; (9) support the musical life of the community and encourage others to do so; and (10) are able to continue their musical learning independently.[23]

These—and a handful of publications like them—are the documents providing the bases for curriculum building in the arts. They establish the standards against which teachers and communities can measure their programs. They furnish the criteria by which programs can be evaluated, representing the points of departure for proposed changes. These standards derive their legitimacy from the fact that they represent what constitutes a good program in the collective judgment of the professionals who have spent their lives working in the various fields of arts education. They also reveal the directions in which education in the arts ought to be moving, in the judgment of those professionals. They are higher standards that those typically found in many communities, but they are achievable.

According to the Council of Chief State School Officers, 36 states provide curriculum guidelines and supplementary materials in art, 34 do in music, 20 do in theater and 18 do in dance.[24] These materials vary enormously in their specificity and in their helpfulness. Some are excellent. Others are not. But regardless of how good the state guidelines are, each district must develop its own curriculum in each of the arts, and it must organize that curriculum in written form in a curriculum guide.

These guides are typically based on the materials of professional associations, state departments of education and other sources, but their development at the local level is essential because the process of curriculum development itself yields important benefits. The act of writing a curriculum guide requires that the teachers themselves consider carefully what goals they will seek to achieve, what learning experiences will be necessary, what materials and equipment will be needed and how they will know when their goals have been achieved. The curriculum guide provides essential orientation for new teachers, and it functions as a handbook and daily reference source for experienced teachers. The lack of a curriculum guide usually indicates the lack of a well-conceived curriculum.

ASSESSMENTS OF LEARNING

The vehicles for assessing learning in the arts will need to differ from those traditionally used to assess progress in such learning areas as reading, writing and arithmetic. Standard and criterion-referenced tests tend to reflect competency or lack of it in

a narrow range of the curriculum being taught. As discussed below, assessments of learning in an arts curriculum will need to
draw upon trends in qualitative and ethnographic research and
permit more divergent approaches for evaluating student progress
and success.

DETERMINING THE CONTENT OF ARTS CURRICULA

Six essential concerns that states, districts and schools can address
in considering the content of an arts curriculum are formulated hi-
erarchically in the series of questions below. The most global concern is considered first.

1. Which arts?
2. What content at which grade levels?
3. Which management approach for an arts curriculum?
4. Which strategy of delivery within each discipline?
5. Which type of lesson formats?
6. Which means of assessment?

WHICH ARTS?

Will the curriculum within a district or school focus on one or
more of the traditionally recognized arts—music, dance, drama,
the visual arts or creative writing? Although each discipline contributes in a unique way to sensing, learning, and re-creating
knowledge and imagery, how much time can schools devote to
more than one of the arts and do the job well?[25]

Included in the concern of "which arts" is the concomitant issue of "whose arts." Within each discipline will western culture
be emphasized or will other cultural and historical viewpoints be
covered as well? The College Board suggests that the relatively
narrow focus on studying the arts of Western Europe and the
United States threatens excellence in arts instruction in two ways.
First, because students are presented with a restricted view of arts
themes, styles and cultural influences, their knowledge of the arts
is less rich and complex than it could be. Second, students belong-
ing to groups whose arts have not been traditionally studied,
such as South Americans, Africans, Asians and minority Americans, do not have the opportunity to see arts produced by people
from their own cultures and to experience possible role-model effects.[26]

The task of selecting "which arts" becomes discouraging because of the volume and variety of materials available and the way in which the literature has classified them: "Some texts treat each art separately; some discuss them together; some treat material historically, some by the themes with which they deal, some by stylistic trends."[27] One suggestion, therefore, is to organize instruction through the study of exemplars in the various arts disciplines.[28] Because exemplars are highlights in the stages of a civilization, they provide a common base of imagery for all to share. Language, thought and feeling are influenced by the study of exemplars and are subsequently transmitted to others whenever they are encountered in the culture. The benefit of this suggested curriculum is that students would share in a common cultural, historical and visual literacy.

WHAT CONTENT?

The decision on the specific arts content at each grade level, creating an ideal sequence of instruction for grades K-12, is based on two major considerations. The first is to identify the knowledge, skills or processes embedded in the content itself so that the content can be both understood and re-created. The second is to identify the stages of thinking at which knowledge, skills or processes should be introduced and taught so that they can be best and most easily learned. The second consideration is based on knowledge of child development, learning theories and cognitive approaches.

Both considerations—how to outline the content and when to teach specific parts of the content—are strongly influenced by two additional concerns. One is the approach the school or district takes in arts curriculum management, discussed below, and the second is responsibility for the approach. For instance, the Arizona Department of Education recently outlined a Visual Arts Sequenced Curriculum Guide for elementary classroom teachers, grades 1 through 6.[29] Having adopted a discipline-based approach to visual arts education developed by The Getty Center for Education in the Arts,[30] the state needed separate curriculum outlines for creative arts expression, aesthetic assessment and the study of past and present art and artists for the six grade levels. For example, to help first and second graders observe and represent their environment, they were assigned the task of making a painting of handmade or manufactured objects commonly found in the house or of making a sculpture from such materials as egg cartons, string, cardboard cylinders and other throw-away, mass-produced items. The same curriculum goal—to produce art as a representation of one's environment—was tailored to fifth and sixth graders, who had to choose from such tasks as designing clothes, magazine layouts, houses or the decor of a room.

WHICH MANAGEMENT APPROACH?

The management approach adopted is often referred to as the conceptual base of the curriculum. The conceptual base comprises the theory, rationale, historical perspective and research applications that have contributed to forming the curriculum. In the visual arts there are three general approaches to curriculum management: (1) a creative self-expression approach (also termed the traditional approach[31] or a nondirective approach[32]), (2) a competency-based approach and (3) a discipline-based arts education approach (DBAE).

The creative approach has been the general domain of the arts teacher, whose role has been to create interest, motivate and encourage children to use and produce art as a means of self-expression and creativity. In one view, the most important aspect of art education in the elementary classroom is art as a creative means of self-expression.[33] Because the creative process is the essential concern, the curriculum focuses mainly on production aspects of the visual arts—hands-on activities that produce unique art products. The curriculum content, therefore, is strongly influenced by the total experience and design choices of the individual arts teacher in any district or school.

A competency-based approach, like a discipline-based approach, has a written curriculum or guide outlining specific skills and competencies to be gained by students in any particular subject for any grade level, K-12. Second, a competency-based approach tends to narrow the focus of the curriculum to the learning of discrete elements within the specified content. Each element has a specific yardstick, agreed upon by the educational community beforehand, and usually expressed as 70 or 80 percent mastery in such-and-such a skill or competency.

Competency-based programs usually take a number of years to evolve because curriculum workers have to work out decisions on the specific elements within the discipline they feel are most suitable to teach (and learn) at specific grade levels. Then measures of assessment—whether they are competency-based tests generated within the school system, nationwide standardized tests or criterion-referenced tests—can be introduced to determine what students have learned. One state took nine years to develop its 778-page curriculum guide for an articulated arts program from elementary to high school. Within the plan, 206 concepts were identified, and these became the basis for the development of competency-based lessons.[34]

The distinguishing feature of the discipline-based arts education approach to the visual arts is that a balanced emphasis is given to four disciplines: art history, art production, art criticism and aesthetics. The curriculum is written, sequential and carried out school or district wide. In contrast to the traditional approach, the regular classroom teacher can share in the arts education process. In those districts which are staffed by arts specialists, the DBAE approach can be coordinated or implemented by them. The classroom teacher can then share in a collaborative role to implement one or several areas of emphasis under guidance by the arts specialist. In those districts lacking arts specialists at the elementary grades, the general classroom teacher with proper training, continuous inservice, and curriculum material could implement the DBAE program approach. The goals of learning in this approach shift from creative self-expression to studying art so as to become an enlightened consumer, learning what art has transmitted across cultures.

In a DBAE approach through the grades, curriculum modules would be planned to balance the learning contribution from each of the four disciplines. At some grade-level clusters, the accent may be on two or three of the disciplines.[35] At times, two disciplines, such as art criticism and aesthetic perception, may be covered in unison. At other times, work in one of the arts can be integrated with other aspects of the curriculum. This would occur, for instance, if painters and their genre were covered in a social studies unit addressing the same historical period. Students would see in artwork how artists portrayed the times and people of that culture. Similarly, art production can easily be recaptured in the language arts classroom. Once students have actually experienced production—"doing," in which most of the physical senses were engaged—they have the raw material for re-creating the experience in their compositions, essays and reports.

It has been argued that the skills of aesthetic perception or aesthetic scanning should take preference over those of art expression in the elementary grades, because such perceptual training "can be regarded as a general approach to aesthetic education, for it is directed toward the perception of the properties that all aesthetic objects exhibit in one medium or another without fusing or confusing the media."[36] The strength of such a focus in the early grades is that aesthetic scanning can be taught through the use of any media. It requires little creative arts talent on the part of the regular classroom teacher, and it provides for concept and vocabulary expansion, leading eventually to a storehouse of language and imagery shared by all.

On the other hand, the College Board suggests that to be ready for college entry, high-school students need intensive work in at least one of the arts, such as the visual arts, theater, music or dance.[37] Such intensive work will provide students with the unique concepts and modes of thinking that are available through that art form. However, within the one arts discipline, students need an equal amount of work in the activities spelled out in a DBAE approach: knowledge of how to produce or perform in that area; knowledge of how to analyze, interpret and evaluate works of art; and knowledge of art in periods, cultures and contexts of history.

WHICH STRATEGY?

One persistent issue is how to structure the content—the lesson material itself—for the classroom. Will the material be delivered initially in whole contexts, with the specific objective of the lesson growing out of the whole? Or will the focus of the presentation be on the specific objective first, with connection to the whole provided later by the teacher or inferentially left for students to generate?

Since the 1970s educators concerned with the development of written literacy among the nation's youngsters have expressed more concern about discovering the processes of reading and writing than about ascertaining the performance of readers and writers. These educators endorse a holistic or whole language approach to written literacy instruction, focusing on a process perspective, meaningful language contexts and the value of language interaction.

On the other hand, the schools continue to conduct written language instruction in which specific skills included in the processes of reading and writing are isolated and taught as ends in themselves. The latter practice perpetuates itself because it is strongly buttressed by traditional evaluation procedures (marketed as standardized and criterion-referenced tests), by textbook and skillbook formats and by such recurring educational ripples as accountability, basic skills, management and mastery. In this approach, reading and writing are viewed as discrete units of measurable skills. Many believe that the mastery of a basic skill facilitates mastery of a higher level skill. The question remains, however, whether understanding or appreciating a whole work could ever equal the sum total of working through a collection of its parts.

Language programs with a holistic emphasis have four essential characteristics:[38]

1. The sequence of instruction moves from the largest unit of language to the smallest so that the whole can fuse the connections of its parts.

2. The largest unit of language used to communicate a meaning affects the meaning. The purpose, direction and intent of a discourse—the complete message unit, such as a short story, poem, play, a lecture, a journal entry, an ad—supersedes the individual meanings of its parts such as paragraphs, sentences and words. A discourse also has verbal and nonverbal features in that the receptive and expressive components of verbal language—listening, speaking, reading and writing—are linked to nonverbal representation (imagery) and conceptualization (composing).

3. Synthesis is encouraged in a holistic approach. Synthesis entails establishing relations among common and uncommon elements and requires a search for connectedness on the part of each individual student. It is a networking of connections. Such thinking occurs, for instance, during the composing of a musical piece, in which new notes and movements are arranged and rearranged to bring about a particular feeling and sense of fulfillment about the total composition. It occurs during writing, when the writer composes sentences with particular word arrangements that convey the message the writer is visualizing. Synthesis requires the higher thought processes of evaluating, justifying, classifying, grouping and perceiving how things are alike or different.

4. Language is used in meaningful ways and in real social contexts. Beginning writers are encouraged to write for meaning and purpose as a means to interact and communicate with peers in classroom environments rather than to study and practice written language conventions. In this social

context, the learning of language accompanies the use of language, with increasing facility in transforming language structures in different ways, on different occasions and for different audiences.

The general characteristics of instruction in specific skills (parts-specific instruction) and of holistic approaches have been presented to the arts education community because the same issues touch the question of how the arts can be managed for instructional delivery. Any of the three general approaches discussed earlier—traditional, competency-based, or discipline-based, can present specific arts topics sequenced for instruction from either a holistic or a parts-specific perspective. As suggested earlier, however, a competency-based approach favors parts-specific instruction because the criterion is mastery of specific objectives.

There is a danger if the objectives become too specific. As curriculum specialists set goals for a sequenced curriculum, they need to resist the temptation of exercising too much logic in defining all the parts of a singular arts topic. If the parts are broken down too thoroughly, discrete exercises may be generated to teach the parts, and evaluation instruments may be constructed to ascertain whether the parts have been learned.

For example, the concept of "line" as it applies to drawing or painting in the visual arts can be taught in distinct ways. If the goal is the learning of the names of different kinds of lines and how they look in representation, a work page can be generated. Children can see the words used to describe the representation and can practice the strokes on the work page. Once the lesson ends, evaluation can take place at any time thereafter to ascertain whether the specific names of line strokes have been learned. A more holistic approach would encompass the teacher's modeling or showing what lines do to a particular art product. The focus might be the initial use of one or several artworks produced by "exemplars" in which the quality of "line" affected the quality of meaning. While children see the teacher model a drawing or point to lines on an artwork, they hear the appropriate vocabulary and language used in the context of an actual work. Children might then practice making different kinds of lines by using a variety of media, such as pencils, crayons, felt pens, spray paint, tempera paint. This practice, starting as a controlled one, may evolve into one in which experimentation and free expression are encouraged. Then youngsters can be exposed to other works of visual art in which lines are used in different ways to communicate both mean-

ing and feeling. Children could then become aesthetically engaged
by bringing their views and developing perceptions to evaluate
and appreciate how line transmits particular effects.

WHICH TYPE OF LESSON FORMAT?

Two strategies have been identified: a directive strategy, which
gives students the components of a skill or task from the outset,
and an inductive strategy, which helps students articulate for
themselves the key attributes of that skill.[39] Teachers can vary the
two strategies to suit the demands of the content and students'
ability levels. When a skill is complex and students require step-
by-step guidance, the teacher would be wise to use the steps of
the directive strategy. When a teacher wants students to infer and
think through the demands of the process, an inductive strategy
may be more appropriate.

It would appear that in the discipline of arts production or arts
expression, the inductive approach would be most useful. Here,
students would experiment with a craft, style or skill, reflect upon
what they have learned and apply the skill or knowledge in future
arts lessons. This inductive base may also help them to criticize,
appreciate and critically study art of other artists and periods. On
the other hand, the directive strategy would seem to be most useful in the disciplines of aesthetic evaluation, art criticism and art
study because learners have to be shown what to do and look for
in each of these domains.

It has been maintained that aesthetic perception requires formal instruction: ''Good thinking requires abstraction from the concrete particularity of the object; aesthetic perception requires the
apprehension of this particularity.''[40] Teacher modeling in the directive approach through an articulated curriculum would be a
means of teaching learners how to apprehend the particulars.

WHICH MEANS OF ASSESSMENT?

Evaluation is the key component in establishing legitimacy for
arts curricula, and possibly this concern should have been high-
lighted first. Regardless of the conceptual approach, evaluation
will need to be considered as the curriculum is evolving, not as an
afterthought when the curriculum is ready to be implemented or
in place.

A problem arises in the design and selection of evaluation instruments. Evaluation must assess the thinking and learning processes generated in a program. Evaluation in the arts cannot follow

traditional standardized procedures adopted by states and districts, because the arts, especially if approached with a holistic emphasis, foster higher level thinking: application, analysis, synthesis
and evaluation. Standardized testing generally measures the two
lowest domains of cognitive inquiry, knowledge and comprehension. Thus, even with the best of arts programs, districts would be
shortchanging the thinking capability of their students if they evaluated them solely through short-answer, written literacy items.

Furthermore, the higher level thought processes of the cognitive taxonomy subsume lower ones.[41] Students engaged in aesthetic perception and art criticism, by the very nature of the
disciplines, are operating at the highest level of cognitive inquiry.
They evaluate by using external and internal criteria to form judgments. This evaluation subsumes knowledge and comprehension
of art forms, period and style, and the ability to analyze a work
with a critical, appreciative eye. Rather than answer a paper-and-
pencil item on a knowledge-based test, the student, during the
telling or writing of an aesthetic scanning activity, tells who the
artist was, his or her style and attributes and the artist's moment
in history.

Those designing evaluations of arts content and disciplines for
districts and states will need to be open-minded and imaginative,
possibly employing the techniques of qualitative or ethnographic
research—the study of subjects' behavior in their natural environment. In this case the environment would be that of classrooms in
which arts activities are generated. Among the assessment tools of
ethnographic research that could apply to discipline-based arts
programs are observation, written accounts of student performance, and interview.

Districts could also apply some traditional assessment techniques to work produced in, or as a consequence of, an arts class.
For instance, during an oral discourse by a student engaged in
aesthetic assessment or art criticism, the teacher may follow a
checklist of items in the curriculum supplied by the district. As the
student evaluates an artwork, the teacher checks off items as they
are mentioned and could then ask questions about any items on
the list that were not volunteered by the student. Mastery of 70 to
80 percent could be established as passing criteria.

At higher grade levels, a written report or composition relating
to any of the arts disciplines could be required of students. The
report could be scored or evaluated with the use of a holistic rat-
ing scale.[42] Such scales traditionally assess unity, coherence, style
or imagination, transition and mechanics. However, a section for

content could easily be added to the scoring weights. Students involved in art expression or art history could be asked to write reports on a semiannual or annual basis as a means of conveying
their knowledge of the discipline. If a student cannot make a piece
of artwork with great skill, he or she may be able to write about it
well.

With both the oral checklist and written paper designs suggested above, districts could go beyond informal evaluations to
reach formal assessments. A pool of evaluators drawn from the
teaching staff could be trained in the evaluation techniques. Using
practice students' works, the evaluators would develop ''standardized'' instruments, so that if two evaluators go to sixth-grade classes in two different schools, they measure student competency
within a reliable range of agreement.

Not all students at any one grade level need be evaluated. The
district could randomly select one set of students and track their
growth over several years' time. Another group of randomly selected students could be compared with a control group population to see if the arts curriculum is indeed increasing learning in
arts production, aesthetic perception, or oral and written language
proficiency. Thus, the task of conducting evaluations would bring
together teachers, arts specialists, artists, scholars and critics.[43]

ACHIEVING THE GOALS OF ARTS EDUCATION

During the past 20 years arts educators have been delighted to see
the creation of state and local arts agencies and various national
advocacy organizations. As individuals and as organizations, educators and advocates have worked together at every opportunity
and at every level to achieve the objectives they hold in common.

However, arts educators have been distressed in recent years
to note indifference and even hostility on the part of some alleged
arts advocates toward instructional programs rooted in various individual arts. It has been implied from time to time, for example,
that the present system of arts education is a failure and the teachers are unqualified. This is simply not true. The system has its
faults, but it is certainly not a failure. No other system in the
world has so successfully brought the arts to large numbers of
young people. Though some teachers are inadequate, the percent-
age is probably lower than in other fields.

Arts educators are also offended by the idea that it is more important for a student to have experience in something called "the arts" than it is actually to learn one of the arts disciplines, and by the idea that the state and local arts agencies are the institutions best qualified to provide guidance and leadership with respect to policy concerning arts education. Some arts advocates seem to think that arts education was invented shortly after the National Endowment for the Arts was created in 1965. The fact is that music has been taught in school since the time of Plato, and it was officially introduced as a part of the curriculum in the public schools of the United States in Boston in 1837. Music education is celebrating its sesquicentennial anniversary in U.S. schools this year.

Arts advocates sometimes seem to have a distorted view of the role of the federal government. As a result of support at the local level and, to a lesser extent, the state level, arts programs have existed in the schools for generations. The federal government played almost no role. Yet in 1983 advocacy sources told a committee of the House of Representatives that "without the vital encouragement of the arts at the federal level, the arts in the schools have quickly disappeared as a necessary part of the educational process at the state and local levels."[44] This is nonsense. Such statements reveal that the speaker is completely out of touch with the reality of arts education.

What can arts advocates do to promote and advance arts education? First of all, they can support the nation's arts teachers, most of whom feel that they receive little support from the arts community, the education community or anyone else. Second, they can fight aggressively to strengthen and expand the arts programs that already exist throughout the nation but which, for some mysterious reason, seem to be largely ignored by arts advocates. Third, they can work vigorously to introduce arts programs in those schools where none currently exists. To be effective, however, these activities must be coordinated with the efforts of the professional arts educators; otherwise nothing will happen because there will be no qualified professionals to follow through.

By far the greatest potential contribution of arts advocates lies in lobbying and helping to persuade decision makers at every level to include the arts in the curriculum. Arts advocates and the support groups that exist in the typical community have enormous potential to rally support and exert pressure on behalf of the arts programs in the schools. Where were they when educators were suffering cutbacks in the early 1980s? Occasionally they were right there, lobbying with the educators; but too often, astonishingly, they seemed to take no notice.

Arts educators need the help of arts advocates to achieve the following specific goals:

1. Every student at every level must have access to a balanced, sequential, high-quality program of instruction in the arts in school taught by qualified teachers.

2. Approximately 15 percent of the instructional program of every student at every level, K-12, should be devoted to the arts.

3. Every high school should require at least one unit of study in music, art, theater or dance for graduation.

4. Every college or university should require at least one unit of study in music, art, theater or dance for admission.

5. Every prospective elementary classroom teacher should have at least 12 semester hours of credit in methods and materials for teaching the arts.

Lobbying should be directed to the individual or group with the authority to act in each of these matters. Sometimes it will be the state legislators or the governor. In other cases it will be the state superintendent or the commissioner of education or the state board of education. In still other cases it will be the local superintendent or board of education or the various faculties of the university. If lobbying is unsuccessful with one source, usually others can be approached. What is important is to work together and to keep trying.

The need for universal access to arts instruction and for adequate time for the arts should be given the highest priority in these efforts. Anyone genuinely interested in arts education should twist the arm of every decision maker at both state and local levels to achieve these goals. What specific actions are needed to ensure high-quality arts programs and sufficient time for the arts in every school? Who has the authority to take these actions? What arguments are likely to be most effective? Who can help make the most effective case? The answers to these questions constitute a blueprint for action.

There are many other things arts advocates can do to support and safeguard arts programs in schools. They must call the attention of the public to ill-advised policies or proposals that will adversely affect instruction. They must alert the public to beware, for example, of proposed revenue-limitation measures such as Proposition 13 and Proposition 2-1/2. And whenever reductions in school support are unavoidable, they must help ensure that the burden does not fall disproportionately on the arts. They must beware, too, of increases in the requirements for high-school graduation without increases in the number of periods in the school day. Invariably, the result is that students are less able to fit the arts into their schedules. It is almost impossible to offer an adequate arts program in a six-period day, but why should the day have only six periods? Should the curriculum be designed to fit the schedule or should the schedule be designed to fit the curriculum?

Arts advocates must also beware of optional honors diplomas, such as one in Virginia. The pressures from from peers and parents to seek such a diploma are enormous, and the result is that students have less time to elect arts courses. They must beware of academic eligibility requirements, such as one in Texas, where only after two years of strenuous effort did the state recognize the obvious—that credit-bearing arts courses are by definition not extracurricular. They must beware of the side-effects of seemingly innocuous proposals, such as one in Indiana to reduce elementary class size, which in many schools led to the loss of the music room for another section of third grade.

Advocates must beware of testing programs that are unbalanced and that fail to recognize that the arts belong among the basics. They must beware of arts magnet schools when they permit a reduced commitment to the arts in the other schools of the district. They must beware of state department of education guidelines, such as those in Georgia in 1985, limiting instruction in music and 13 other subjects to not more than 110 clock hours each in grades 6 through 8 combined. And they must beware of bizarre legislation with superficial and simplistic provisions, such as that in Iowa providing a bounty of $50 to every school district for every secondary student who enrolls in an advanced course in science or math.

All arts advocates need to become aware of what is happening to the arts programs in their own states and local school districts. It is up to them to serve as the watchdogs—growling, barking, and even biting, if necessary—to ensure that the schools offer arts programs that are balanced, rigorous and high in quality.

TAKING STOCK

What are the strengths and weaknesses of contemporary arts education? There is more evidence in music than in the other arts, and in these matters the arts may be similar. The strength of music education today is that large numbers of capable and imaginative teachers from one end of this nation to the other are doing a remarkably good job, often under difficult circumstances. The quality of instruction has never been higher than it is at this moment. The weakness is that not nearly enough students are being reached. The quality is up from 15 years ago, but the quantity is down. Far too many elementary schools have no music specialists whatever, or have too few. Far too many high schools offer only one band and chorus. And far too many teachers are responsible for far too many students.

Of course, a few arts teachers are simply not doing a good job, and a few arts programs deserve to be eliminated. But the overwhelming majority of arts teachers in the schools are capable, well-qualified and enthusiastic. They know what to do; that is not the problem. What is needed now is more staff, more time and more support.

Working together, arts advocates and educators can make a difference. Instead of wringing their hands, preaching to small groups of the already committed and complaining about the terrible condition of arts education, they should begin today to bring pressure on school officials in all 50 states and all 15,398 school districts. This pressure should aim at strengthening the arts programs that exist, adding arts programs where they do not exist and supporting the 133,000 arts teachers who are struggling every day against enormous odds to bring to reality the vision all share of a high-quality program of instruction in the arts in school for every young American.

Notes

1. Because of the divergent perspectives of the authors, and because of the circumstances under which this paper was prepared, it is not in fact a collaboration but rather a composite of sections, each prepared entirely by one of the authors. "Delineating the Roles of The Arts Curriculum" (except point 5), and "Determining the Content of Arts Curricula," are the work of Professor Sinatra. "Appraising the State

of the Arts in Schools," "Identifying Assumptions About Arts Education," "Delineating the Roles of the Arts Curriculum" (point 5 only), "Achieving the Goals of Arts Education" and "Taking Stock" are the work of Professor Lehman. Neither author should be assumed to share responsibility for the views of the other.

2. *A Trend Study of High School Offerings and Enrollments: 1972-73 and 1981-82* (Washington: National Center for Educational Statistics, 1984), 31, 39, 47, 55.

3. Council of Chief State School Officers, *Arts, Education and the States: A Survey of State Education Policies* (Washington: Council of Chief State School Officers, 1985), 6.

4. Daniel V. Steinel, *Arts in Schools: State By State* (Reston, Virginia: Music Educators National Conference, 1985), 1.

5. See, for example, Ernest Boyer, *High School* (New York: Harper & Row, 1983), 97-98; John Goodlad, *A Place Called School* (New York: McGraw-Hill Book Co., 1983), 134-36, 286-87; Mortimer Adler, *The Paideia Proposal* (New York: Macmillan Publishing Co., 1982), 22-24; The College Board, *Academic Preparation for College* (New York: The College Board, 1983), 16-18.

6. Goodlad, *A Place Called School*, 134-136.

7. Ibid., 286-87.

8. The College Board, *Academic Preparation for College*; Council of Chief State School Officers, *Arts, Education and the States*.

9. R. V. Bullough and S. L. Goldstein, "Technical Curriculum Form and American Elementary School Art Education," *Journal of Curriculum Studies*, 16 (1984):144.

10. Ibid., 143-154.

11. E. L. Boyer, "Art as Language: Its Place in the Schools," in *Beyond Creating: The Place for Art in America's Schools*, Getty Center for Education in the Arts (Los Angeles: The J. Paul Getty Trust, 1985).

12. I. S. Kirsch and A. Jungeblut, *Literacy: Profiles of America's Young Adults* (NAEP Report No. 16-PL-02) (Princeton, New Jersey: Educational Testing Service, 1986).

13. R. C. Sinatra, *Visual Literacy Connections to Thinking, Reading and Writing* (Springfield, Illinois: Charles C. Thomas, 1986).

14. E. P. Torrance, "Creativity and Its Educational Implications," in *Educating the Ablest*, J. Gowan, J. Khatena, and E. Torrance, eds. (Itasca, Illinois: Peacock Publishing Co., 1979).

15. Ibid.

16. J. C. Gowan, J. Khatena, and E. P. Torrance, *Educating the Ablest: On the Education of Gifted Children* (Itasca, Illinois: Peacock Publishing Co., 1979).

17. H. S. Broudy, "A Common Curriculum in Aesthetics and Fine Arts," in *Individual Differences and the Common Curriculum* (Eighty-second Yearbook of the National Society for the Study of Education, Part I), G. D. Fenstermacher and J. I. Goodlad, eds. (Chicago: University of Chicago Press, 1983), 219-47.

18. E. W. Eisner, *The Role of Discipline-Based Art Education in America's Schools* (Los Angeles: Getty Center for Education in the Arts, 1987), 6.

19. N. Postman, "The Ascent of Humanity: A Coherent Curriculum," *Educational Leadership*, 37 (1980):300-3.

20. The College Board, *Academic Preparation for College*.

21. *The School Music Program: Description and Standards* (2nd ed.: Reston, Virginia: Music Educators National Conference, 1986).

22. *Purposes, Principles, and Standards for School Art Programs* (Reston, Virginia: National Art Education Association, n.d.).

23. *The School Music Program*, 13-14.

24. Council of Chief State School Officers, *Arts Education and the States*, 18.

25. Ibid. A survey conducted by the Council of Chief State School Officers shows that visual art and music top the states' curriculum list.

26. The College Board, *Academic Preparation for College*.

27. Broudy, "A Common Curriculum," 240.

28. Ibid.

29. Arizona Department of Education, *Visual Arts Sequenced Curriculum Guide: Grades 1-6* (Phoenix: Arizona Department of Education, 1985).

30. Getty Center for the Arts, *Beyond Creating: The Place for Art in America's Schools* (Los Angeles: J. Paul Getty Trust, 1985).

31. M. D. Day, "Evaluating Student Achievement in Discipline-Based Art Programs," *Studies in Art Education*, 26 (1985), 232-240.

32. Council of Chief State School Officers, *Arts, Education and the States*.

33. According to M. D. Day, a strong conceptual base for the traditional arts approach was provided by V. Lowenfeld, in *Creativity and Mental Growth* (New York: Macmillan, 1947), and later by V. Lowenfeld and L. Brittain, *Creative and Mental Growth*, 7th ed. (New York: Macmillan, 1982). See Day, "Evaluating Student Achievement in Discipline-Based Art Programs", 232-40.

34. Bullough and Goldstein, "Technical Curriculum Form." According to a recent survey conducted by the Council of Chief State School Officers, competency-based programs involve an extensive period of preparation in which states have five to eight years to implement an approved program. Council of Chief State School Officers, *Arts, Education and the States*.

35. Arizona Department of Education, *Visual Arts Sequenced Curriculum Guide*.

36. Broudy, "A Common Curriculum," 233. See also, H. S. Broudy, "Curriculum Validity in Art Education," *Studies in Art Education*, 26 (1985):212-15.

37. The College Board, *Academic Preparation for College*.

38. R. C. Sinatra, "Holistic Applications in Computer-based Reading and Language Arts Programs," in *The Computer in Reading and Language Arts*, G. Mason and J. Blanchard, eds. (New York: Haworth Press, 1987).

39. B. K. Beyer, "Practical Strategies for the Direct Teaching of Thinking

Skills,'' in *Developing Minds: A Resource Book for Teaching Thinking*, A. Costa, ed. (Alexandria, Virginia: Association for Supervision and Curriculum Development, 1986), 145-50.

40. Broudy, ''A Common Curriculum,'' 232.

41. Levels as defined by: B. S. Bloom, ed., *Taxonomy of Educational Objectives: Cognitive Domain* (New York: David McKay, 1956).

42. Such scales have been proposed by P. B. Diederich, *Measuring Growth in English* (Urbana, Illinois: National Council of Teachers of English, 1974), and R. C. Sinatra and J. Venezia, ''A Visual Approach to Improved Literacy Skills for Special Adolescents,'' *The Exceptional Child*, 33 (1986):187-92.

43. Broudy, ''A Common Curriculum,'' 219-247.

44. ''The Interrelationship of Funding for the Arts at the Federal, State, and Local Levels,'' *Eighteenth Report of the Committee on Government Operations, House Report 98-547* (November 15, 1983), U.S. House of Representatives, 29.

Charles Dorn and Lonna Jones

PROMOTING PARTNERSHIPS FOR ARTS EDUCATION: TEACHERS, ARTISTS AND SCHOLARS

P artnerships in the 1980s—those on behalf of arts education as well as other school subjects—have aimed at helping schools with content reforms. Business and education alliances for strengthening mathematics, science and reading are only a few years old. Arts and education alliances, on the other hand, have been testing partnership notions for some 20 years. Perhaps no other area of the curriculum can record so many attempts to incorporate the notion of partnership, and the partners themselves, into the curriculum.

ASSESSING PAST AND PRESENT PARTNERSHIPS

School arts programs have often been characterized not only by long-standing and productive associations with nonprofit organizations and community resources, but also by an emphasis on partnerships at the school site, so that children might benefit directly. One theme that stands out in the public record of collaborations on behalf of arts education over the last three decades is the explicit and consistent intent to bring artists and academics (defined variously) into working arrangements with the formal education system. This aim was first promoted by artists and academics themselves, then by administrators who devised program strategies. The idea of artists in schools, not surprisingly, found early and enthusiastic backing from scientists; an example is this statement from a prestigious national panel of the President's Science Advisory Committee in 1964:

> Having musicians in the schools would be good for education and good for the musicians. Such an effort would work to stop the growing alienation of the musical profession from American life and education. Of course, techniques for coping with teacher-certification requirements

would have to be worked out. . . . Having resident musi-
cians in the schools makes economic as well as pedagogical
sense in a way that having resident scientists in the school
does not.[1]

In the 1960s government agencies and foundations, taking their
cues from various conferences and reports, encouraged partnerships as fertile avenues toward rapprochement within the arts education field. Later, in the 1970s, these funding sources backed
such alliances in part as accommodations to school conditions.

As partnerships were promoted, so they were judged. The
public record shows that the thousands of collaborations of artists
and teachers, the hundreds of collaborations of academics, artists
and teachers, and the scores of mechanisms that facilitated their
communication were assessed, to some degree, on the basis of
their value (1) as personal support systems and (2) as unified
fronts against common dangers from straitened school budgets,
falling enrollments, inflation and the emphasis on narrowly defined "basics." The record is marked by personal and anecdotal
testimony supporting beliefs, emotions, perceptions and not necessarily disparate viewpoints: the self-acclaimed mavericks who
stressed the value of "doing" the arts; the stylish and richly publi-
cized arguments for infusing, integrating and interrelating the arts
with or into all education; the fundamental analysis of the arts qua
arts, with improved, sequential curricula equal in status to the traditional academic degree and subjects, and with practice under
skilled tutelage in formal educational settings; and the eloquent es-
pousal of the arts as modes of thought, languages of discourse and
ways of knowing, at least equal in importance to other means of
communication, such as letters and numbers and mathematical
symbols.

In some cases, yesterday's experiments with the means and
mechanisms for communication turned into today's routines. Although advocates do not assemble today with the same missionary
zeal described in reports from the 1960s, they convene nonethe-
less. Unfortunately, administrators continue as the principal players in devising partnership strategies, as they were in the 1970s.
Teachers, artists and academics cross institutional and personal
boundaries more readily today than 20 years ago. The phrase "artists in schools" speaks for itself in programs of elementary schools
and specialized arts high schools. As often as financially possible,
artists and performers are on site at many schools, and such arrangements are initiated more often today by the schools them-

selves than by support groups. In elementary and middle schools, the presence and contributions of artists are explained variously, with emphasis on developing the whole child rather than the whole arts curriculum.

"Artists in schools" is less descriptive of secondary school ties to the arts community; on-site residencies and performances have always been far less common at this level of education. This is not to say, however, that students and arts teachers in many public and private high schools do not seek out and maintain institutional and personal connections with artists and scholars as part of the instructional program. They do. The few who have written about the impact of arts institutions and artists on the high school arts program have emphasized the students' role in defining connections with these arts resources, and the teacher's role in encouraging the students to search for these connections.

By tradition, partnerships have been defined largely with the general classroom teacher as student of the arts: as such, many partnerships have aimed as much for conversion as instruction. Teachers' conversions are well documented; their progress, however, as evidenced by curriculum, instruction or insights, has not been. Although some artists and teachers have written about their experiences, and a few programs have published anthologies providing more than anecdotal or enthusiastic testimony from poets, writers and other artists, surprisingly few accounts include the views of experienced arts teachers, whether as observers or participants. Broad advocacy aims of past partnerships allowed others to speak for master teachers of the arts and other silent partners. Today, with more and more focus on the arts as they are taught in schools, those with "classroom laboratories" can no longer be minor players in devising agendas for improvement.

IDENTIFYING DIMENSIONS OF
THE LEARNING EXPERIENCE

Resumes of 31 arts teachers who met for a week-long seminar in 1984 showed that many in the group moved continually from the classroom to the studio, stage and research environment—as teachers and artists and students and researchers. All were experienced professionals, recognized repeatedly on the basis of their teaching excellence. Even so, only a few spent time as leaders, consultants, and experts, perhaps training teachers on university campuses during the summer (without recognition or institutional affiliation). And very few cited participation in, or contributions to, policy forums and outcomes.

Obviously, one obstacle to the participation of arts teachers in policy making is the enormous amount of preparation required for good teaching. A master teacher summarized the preparations for teaching creative writing classes in a public arts high school with students grades 7-12:

> To prepare for teaching, I read about 200 books a year, thousands of poems and short stories, and also some critical essays. Depth of knowledge is important. I also view at least 200-300 films and analyze them very closely, and get exposure to others. It is important for my students that I have worked in all the various areas of writing. So I've published a great deal of poetry, a great deal of prose. I primarily write short stories and have published several of those. A familiarity with the market place is important, so I seek publication in magazines, mostly literary magazines, for which I've also written and published criticism and book reviews in a variety of areas. Exposure to and translation of foreign literature—European literature in particular—is important for my writing program. I travel—that's important—and I've translated in French and German and published those translations. These are all essential things that I do to prepare for my students.[2]

Another obstacle to full participation of partners in arts education practice is that teachers and students do not view arts learning in the separate and distinct domains of the artist, historian, and critic. Rather, they test these domains together, on a see-saw between the possible and the actual, between the imaginative and the theoretical and between what might be true and what is. This notion sounds less mystical when teachers explain it:

> The artists [who] preceded these [fifth-grade] students must be as familiar to them as their memory of a favorite aunt. The teacher as historian [is like] a family member who willingly shares pieces of family history with younger members of the clan. The intent is to have each student adopt the whole of history of art as his family, to present art history as fellow family members doing and conquering certain tasks. This use of historical figures in art comes naturally to anyone trained in studio art.[3]

Good arts programming and good educational theory are linked to what professionals in the arts know and do. To provide effective arts education in the schools, artists, scholars and arts teachers should work together as partners in the organic and synergistic educational process. Three major focuses for partnerships of teachers, artists and scholars are: (1) designing and improving the arts curriculum, (2) providing for arts instruction, and (3) preparing teachers for the schools.

IMPROVING THE ARTS CURRICULUM

Those in the arts, both in schools and outside them, generally agree that today's school arts curriculum is inadequately educating students in (1) artistic production and performance, (2) analysis, interpretation and evaluation and (3) historical and cultural knowledge. Few concur, however, about what particular instructional content is essential for effective arts education (nor was there explicit agreement on content in the past).

Educators, artists and scholars in the arts differ on what forms of knowledge are the most critical and on what pedagogical process most effectively transmits this knowledge. Pedagogues tend to approach arts education by first discovering what children can do, then seeking art content most suited to children's needs. Art scholars most often value the canons of the discipline. Artists emphasize the learning conditions conducive to expressive performance and creation. However excellent the reasons for each group's adhering to its own view, without some consensus little change is likely to occur in the school curriculum. A curriculum must take into account both the needs of the learner and the learning conditions considered essential by the artist and the scholar if it is to provide quality arts education.

To effect real change in the current arts curriculum, new structures or procedures must be established to promote partnerships among educators, artists and scholars who respect one another's potential contributions to the evolution of a more viable curriculum. Past efforts have demonstrated that philosophers, artists, historians and critics can work together effectively. But if the goal is to change curricula, arts educators, artists and scholars need to take part directly, from conception through implementation.

PROVIDING BETTER INSTRUCTION

Similar efforts to establish interactive partnerships among educators, artists and scholars are also necessary to provide better arts instruction in the schools. Artists-in-schools programs operating since the mid-1960s have contributed to the quality and definition of arts education programs in many U.S. school systems. New programs should include arts scholars, such as historians and critics, as instructors. Not only do artists, art scholars, historians and critics contribute directly as teachers, but they also provide professional models with whom students can identify. New and more effective approaches need to be developed and evaluated for helping them participate actively—rather than tangentially, as they did in the past—in the instructional process.

PREPARING ARTS TEACHERS

National panels, commissions and state legislatures, though identifying malaise in education, have not offered solutions for effectively educating arts teachers. Nor have related efforts—for example, those by groups seeking to separate pedagogical education from education in the discipline—offered better prospects for improving teacher education in the arts. The real solutions will come from partnerships that focus on the need for better teacher education in the subjects of performance, history, criticism and aesthetics. To achieve this goal, the nature of the education prospective teachers receive in these three areas must change. Merely tinkering with university administrative structures or expanding the number of years of teacher training will not suffice.

To improve the education of arts teachers, the first step is to improve significantly the overall content of the courses offered to prospective teachers in performance, criticism, history, aesthetics and education. Neither experience nor research supports the claim that teaching in the arts is accomplished best by the artist *or* by the child specialist alone. In the past, one extreme or the other has been advocated. It is now time to develop curricula that reflect a true collaboration between artists, teachers and scholars.

Effecting fundamental change within arts teacher education through the combined efforts of the artist, educator and scholar rather than creating the appearance of change through external collaborations of these partners will not be easy. If action is not taken, however, the education of the arts teacher may be left to the political whims of state legislatures or to college and university senates. The immediate task is to enable artists, scholars and educators to work in concert at both the state and university levels, restructuring the arts teacher education programs in universities and colleges. Such an effort will undoubtedly lead to significant changes in the character, content, sequence and scope of the arts teacher education programs in higher education.

ADDRESSING PERSISTENT ISSUES

A number of groups are now advocating that arts curricula be designed with a well-defined content, sequence and scope, giving rise once more to a long-standing question: should efforts be expended to create a single model for the development of the arts curriculum in the school and college? One such movement in the visual arts, stimulated by the J. Paul Getty Trust, has embarked on a major effort to define a common content, sequence and scope for the visual arts curriculum in elementary schools. The rationale for such an effort is, in part, that few published curriculum models are now available, and only a few elementary schools use them. In secondary schools, the visual arts curriculum is a loosely agreed upon set of performance goals considered essential for the education of the creative artist. In some arts disciplines and in some urban and suburban school districts a curriculum may exist, but with little agreement either within or between arts disciplines about the particular content, sequence and scope that are essential.

Because the education of the artist is individualized, and perhaps always will be, little restructuring of eclectic high-school performance curricula is likely to occur. However, arts education in high schools today is moving toward the general arts education of all secondary students. Such an education, as described in the College Board's *Green Book*, includes appreciation of all the arts as well as instruction in one or more art forms in (1) production and performance, (2) analysis, interpretation and evaluation, and (3) historical and cultural knowledge. With more than 20 states now requiring some education in the arts for high school graduation, there is now a serious challenge to the once almost exclusive emphasis on the performance curriculum.

A second persistent issue affecting the teacher-artist-scholar collaboration is whether artists and scholars should be professionally licensed and made directly responsible for the instruction of students in the elementary and secondary schools.

The National Endowment for the Arts' Artists in Education Program has clearly made a case for the artist in the schools; an equally persuasive case could be made for arts scholars. In many schools today artists are directly engaged in instructing students.

Traditionally, however, the artist is not considered legally responsible for the student's education. Legal responsibility rests with licensed teachers who are prepared in approved programs of teacher education through the National Council on Accreditation of Teacher Education (NCATE). Although experience shows that many artists and scholars are effective teachers and that licensing teachers in itself does not guarantee effective teaching, common sense suggests that individuals who understand how learning takes place and who know the content of their field are most likely to succeed as teachers.

Changes in teacher licensing, designed by some state legislatures to blunt the power of colleges of education or, in some southern states, to meet the threat of teacher shortages, are shifting responsibility for the education of schoolchildren. Some school districts are already encouraging the employment of artists, more specifically holders of M.F.A. degrees, as teachers in the schools. Those supervising such individuals have often reported positively about their teaching effectiveness. To achieve permanent or continuing certification or licensure, most of these individuals are required to take advanced courses in pedagogy. That they can achieve certification on the job, however, brings up the question of whether the total commitment to preservice programs for teacher preparation is necessary. At the same time, however, research is lacking on whether or not M.F.A. teachers are effective. Nor is it known whether hiring and training M.F.A.s will constitute a widespread solution to providing arts education or whether it is only a stopgap for certain levels of schooling.

A third persistent issue affecting collaboration is whether arts teachers should be educated at colleges of the arts or at colleges of education. Current public concern about the quality of teachers generally is influencing arts teacher education programs. Some arts education departments in schools of education are adopting the Holmes Group proposal for five, rather than four, years of training before certification; other arts education departments in schools or colleges of fine arts seem to be staying with their current four-year programs. Although an extra year of preparation could enhance the qualifications of prospective arts teachers, past experience with five-year programs in California suggests that school districts may prefer to hire graduates from the four-year institutions to realize salary savings. If five-year programs are adopted in some but not in all teacher education institutions, similar competitive situations might arise between institutions in all 50 states.

At present there is no evidence that students graduating from arts schools or colleges are significantly better teachers than are graduates of colleges of education. Because state certification requirements must be met in both programs, and professional studies must be taken in "approved" teacher education institutions, the patterns of education for arts teachers may vary little between such institutions.

However, the testing of teachers, when they enter the field and as they advance in their careers, emphasizes their mastery of subject matter rather than their pedagogical knowledge. To the extent that historical and technical knowledge of the subject is a necessary condition for employment and for advancement in the arts teaching profession, the training in the arts disciplines at colleges or schools of the arts may be more effective than that provided by colleges of education.

FOSTERING NEW STYLES OF PARTNERSHIPS AMONG TEACHERS, ARTISTS AND SCHOLARS

Today's partnerships attest to arts education as a highly diversified field—in its practitioners, its supporters and its public. Diversity poses certain problems in arriving at common fundamental goals. But often a more real problem is how to allow partnerships to improve arts education practice without constraining schools of arts, organizations or individuals. Today, fewer frivolous schemes are laid at the schoolhouse door, or foisted on arts organizations for that matter. In arts education today, there is less temptation than there was to fashion the curriculum ends around the funding means.

Dollar support notwithstanding, "content projects are tough to fund," according to Dr. Pamela Menke, former director of education at the National Endowment for the Humanities. Dr. Menke made a distinction between "talking content" and "talking about content": "What usually occurred are endless conversations debating the form a course outline may be, but not practical, tangible, palpable discussion about what should be, or is, taught. And the more abstract the concept, the more elusive the common ground."[4]

Somewhat more concrete, however, are experiences with mechanisms for change. Innovation means doing something for the first time, while institutions are well suited for doing things for the millionth time, Jay Galbraith told The Conference Board in 1985. A newsletter amplified Galbraith's remarks:

> There must be a degree of separation between innova-
> tion and day-to-day operations, and that separation has to
> be the right degree that gets an idea out from under nor-
> mal operations, but can bring it back in again when that is
> appropriate. The separation might be accomplished by a
> "greenhouse" or "skunkworks." It might be temporary or
> permanent. It might be within the larger organization or
> outside. It might be based on a structure for a product, on
> physical separation, on a separate funding process, on ad-
> ministration free of the normal controls.[5]

Not that a "skunkworks" is an apt metaphor, but it often describes "new starts" in school arts programs that take place with,
and feed into, day-to-day practice. Often in the past, elementary
schools have developed a second "operation" that often resulted
in a new vision, a plan and curriculum or other content assistance
for classroom teachers which they could use in shaping instructional strategies. At first such operations seemed to be mostly hap-
penstance. Scrutiny revealed, however, that the participating
individuals—artists, teachers and administrators—had in common
an interest in understanding the basis for innovation and change
rather than a stake in being innovators. "Rather than developing
our arts curriculum with the help of artist residencies we could
have followed the state guide," said one elementary school principal. "But then the ownership would rest with the one teacher
who understood the vocabulary; the others might contribute half-
heartedly. This way more than half of the teachers had an invest-
ment in the instructional aspects."[6]

Start-ups are often fueled by partnerships that co-exist with
school practice. But rarely do schools use a similar arrangement to
monitor standards or to improve or evaluate curriculum, instruction or training. Obviously, partnerships are impractical for many
operations at all levels of formal education, given the time con-
straints, the expertise of teaching staff, and the tangle of requirements, even in the arts. Improvement and evaluation are often
tightly structured tasks, often beyond the control of single educational institutions. Still, if improvement is construed as something
more than a one-way street—with initiators or regulators at one
end and implementors at the other—partnerships have a role beyond the initial phase.

In the last 20 years, the notion of partnerships has helped create converts for arts education within school ranks and among the public. Today's colleges and universities, national professional organizations, state agencies, some school districts and even individual public schools have the resources, the flexibility and the capacity to be both standard-bearers *and* visionaries, with all that that implies for their support of the new in arts education—and also of the enduring.

Notes

1. *Innovation and Experiment in Education*, a progress report of the Panel on Educational Research and Development, President's Science Advisory Committee, March, 1964, p. 20-21.
2. Whalen, Thomas. From transcript of group interviews with 31 arts teachers. Seminar of Exploration, Dedham, MA, August, 1984.
3. Capet, Mitje C. An Exploratory Study of Teaching Visual Arts Grades One Through Eight. A doctoral dissertation submitted to the University of California, Los Angeles, 1985.
4. Menke, Pamela. In meeting with author of this paper, 1986.
5. Galbraith, Jay. Remarks summarized in *Behavioral Sciences Newsletter*, Dec. 9, 1985, p. 1.
6. Peterson, Mark. In conversation with author of this paper, March, 1986.

Richard Bell and Jonathan Katz

PROMOTING PARTNERSHIPS FOR ARTS EDUCATION: ORGANIZATIONS, AGENCIES AND INSTITUTIONS

T housands of organizations are currently working in arts education in towns and cities throughout the United States in school
systems, arts agencies, institutions producing arts, universities,
funding sources and community support groups. Many of these
organizations share information, work cooperatively on special
projects and maintain friendly relations with others working in the
field.

Examples of partnerships among individual organizations are
not lacking; what *is* lacking is a comprehensive pattern of collaboration among groups of organizations working to meet the challenges facing the arts education field today. Can the meaning of
being culturally literate be defined? Can the value of achieving cultural literacy be demonstrated? Are the resources available to get
the job done?

Ambivalence toward the need for arts education appears to be
deeply rooted in the American character. Beginning with the
founding fathers, and including the fraternity of today's business
and political leaders, actions on behalf of arts education have been
few and far between. If this is "a nation at risk" regarding the
general state of education, it is "a nation at sea" regarding the
place of arts in the educational enterprise.

The absence of the arts from the curriculum is all but incom-
prehensible, considering that the arts are the only disciplines that
address students' affective learning capacities and are therefore
the only subjects that give concrete form to the study of feelings.
However, the temptation to blame those outside the arts education field for this state of affairs must be resisted. Even the most
expedient-minded citizens might recognize the need for quality
arts education if those engaged in the profession made a consis-
tently compelling case for the value of the arts in everyday life.
Clearly, arts educators have failed to make this case beyond the
borders of the profession they represent.

This paper (1) explores some of the hindrances to the formation of effective collaborations, (2) outlines the qualities that must be present before fruitful partnerships can occur and (3) suggests several strategies for initiating collaboration among those engaged in the field.

EXAMINING THE INFRASTRUCTURE OF ARTS EDUCATION

For any process to have impact on the arts education field as a whole, the complex infrastructure of the field must be taken into account. The following list contains four categories of groups and organizations with a policy interest in arts education in the K-12 public school system. The major participants within each group are also listed.

1. Public Elementary and Secondary Education
   - Specialist arts teachers
   - Generalist teachers teaching the arts
   - Principals
   - Superintendents
   - District and school curriculum supervisors
   - Local school boards
   - State curriculum consultants
   - State boards of education
   - Chief state school officers
   - U.S. Department of Education
2. Arts-in-Education Organizations
   - Artists
   - Arts organizations with educational programs
   - Producing arts organizations
   - Arts education program and service organizations
3. Funding and Support Resources
   - Parents
   - Foundations with arts/education giving policies
   - Corporations with arts/education giving policies
   - Civic organizations
   - Local arts agencies
   - State arts agencies
   - National Endowment for the Arts
4. University and Professional Training Organizations
   - Fine arts deans

- Deans of education
- University arts departments
- University education departments
- Community schools of the arts

All the participants listed above maintain similar sets of inter-dependent relationships. One can sense the resultant complexity by envisioning each person and organization as the center of a circle, with information from all these affiliations coming in to the center and going out to all these affiliations. Effecting a coherent national movement in any direction thus becomes a major challenge.

Because of the variety of groups representing arts and education interests, they have tended over time to divide into 'camps.' The arts teachers' organizations might be viewed as one camp; the state and local arts agencies, another; the educational administrators, another; the program and service organizations, another; the federal agencies, another; and so on. It would probably be fair to say that there is a higher trust level within these camps than between them, if for no other reason than there is greater familiarity with one another's working process. Even within each camp, however, groups have had to differentiate between their organization and all others to represent their particular membership and to raise funds.

Consider the following example. A specialist teacher of an art in an elementary school may be responsible to a principal and a district curriculum supervisor. Supplementary funds supporting the teacher's work may come from a parents' organization, a local arts agency, a state arts agency or a private-sector sponsor, either directly or through the auspices of an arts and education service organization. The teacher may belong to a state chapter of a national service organization for teachers of that art form, and the teacher may also belong to a union. The teacher's inservice requirements are likely to require seminars or courses at an institution of higher education. And the teacher may also be a practicing artist, expanding mastery of the art form, perhaps as a professional.

Unfortunately, the circle of affiliations outlined here is often incomplete. The specialist art teacher might not have a district curriculum supervisor to report to; there may be no local arts agency serving the community, and the parents' organization may have focused its efforts on a reading program. Even more to the point, the local school might not have a specialist art teacher at all.

The fund-raising process further illustrates the complexity of the arts education infrastructure. For example, to underwrite artist fees in a community-based artist and teacher training project, a nonprofit arts organization submits a grant request to a public arts agency. It makes a second grant request to a local foundation for teacher stipends and materials and a third request to a national corporation to underwrite staff and overhead expenses. Each funding source uses different sets of criteria for assessing the proposal: the public arts agency focuses on how the project benefits artists; the foundation attempts to verify the degree to which the project would meet the foundation's giving priorities in education; the corporation looks at the potential employee involvement and its corporate image in the community. All three funders expect the project to be unique and also to be replicable.

Gradually, ideas and language are tailored to meet the criteria of each funding source. Other arts and education organizations are consulted, along with the local school system. Several of these organizations may become active participants and eventually gain a stake in the project. This scenario often results in a project of considerable merit, but it seldom results in a whole that is more than the sum of its parts beyond the life of the project itself.

UNDERSTANDING THE INFRASTRUCTURE OF EDUCATIONAL DECISION MAKING

The infrastructure of educational decision making adds another kind of complexity that must be taken into consideration in developing strategies for collaborations and partnerships. Educational decisions in the United States are made predominantly at the local level by authorities independent of one another. Of the nation's more than 15,000 school systems, only 70 have school populations of more than 10,000 students. Although these 70 systems comprise 23 percent of the public school population, more than three-quarters of our students are spread out among the remaining school districts, each averaging a few thousand pupils.

School decision-making processes and curricular content are affected by factors that vary considerably from locality to locality. These factors include populations served by the district; geographic area covered by the district; funding structure; educational background of parents; educational background of state legislators; school board make-up over a period of years; average age of individuals in the district; tax rates and assessed property value in the district; and cultural, racial and ethnic influences. In addition, local constituents of state and national organizations do not necessarily respond to national agendas. The teacher in the example above, for instance, is an employee of a local educational agency with a curriculum, budget and guidance for outside funding determined predominantly by that agency.

The arts education field is fragmented because the groups within it have diverse orientations, goals and agendas. Some have broad concerns in education, of which the arts are a part. Others have broad concerns in the arts, of which education is a part. Some focus primarily on producing arts programs in educational settings. Others focus entirely on arts education.

The potential for achieving greater clarity of vision and unity of purpose is further thwarted by the complexity and diversity that characterize the major types of organizations in the field: differences in function and style between the public and private sectors; among national, state and local agencies; between arts organizations and educational institutions; and within the worlds of higher education, and elementary and secondary education. The absence of a common mission, agenda for action or even a shared vocabulary among these organizations inevitably results in a failure to communicate, both among arts educators and between them and those they seek to convince that more and better arts education is needed.

IDENTIFYING REQUISITES
FOR SUCCESSFUL PARTNERSHIPS

The most effective partnerships are among organizations that have assessed their participation from the perspective of enlightened self-interest. A general commitment to the idea of entering collaborative projects will not suffice. No matter how worthy the undertaking, if the partnership does not further the organization's program individually, the relationship will not prosper.

On the other hand, too great a reliance on achieving individual results may obscure the primary reason for working collaboratively with other agencies and institutions—to accomplish what one cannot do alone.

The prerequisites for successful collaborations apply to the arts and education as they do to other fields. Each interested party should have identified its own goals and objectives. Cooperating parties should clarify common and independent interests, identifying the problems that are larger than those they can overcome separately. In general, parties cooperate when they expect that the payoffs from working together will be greater than those ensuing from their individual efforts. Finally, cooperation is more likely to take place when parties trust the leadership advocating cooperation.

The extent to which an organization is capable of entering the world of a partner—first through understanding, next by developing empathy for the partner's perspective and finally by embracing the partner's goals and aspirations—will determine the effectiveness of the partnership. Arts organizations should view themselves also as educational agents; educational institutions should serve also as artistic entities; public agencies and private organizations should encourage projects that complement one another's programs, sometimes sacrificing the prestige associated with being "the first" or with developing the model program for the sake of meeting a genuine need in a particular situation. And finally, if national and state institutions function with a more local perspective, local organizations will be more likely to develop a greater national perspective.

DETERMINING GOALS OF ARTS EDUCATION THAT REQUIRE CONCERTED ACTION

Most of the groups with specific interests in arts education are now identifying issues and goals that require concerted action. It remains for them to convince the arts constituencies and the education constituencies at the local level of the benefits that achieving these goals can bring to them. The incentive for individual organizations to invest in this communication and persuasion is great because they cannot achieve their goals individually.

The aims of arts education in grades K-12 include the following:

1. Making arts education understood as part of basic education

2. Developing and adopting sequential curricula in arts disciplines

3. Providing arts specialist teachers for every school

4. Making inservice arts education training available to teachers, administrators and artists

5. Offering training that emphasizes (a) the intrinsic value of the arts and (b) the integration of the arts into other curriculum areas

6. Providing opportunities such as summer schools, magnet schools and after-school arts instruction for artistically gifted or inclined students

7. Implementing effective evaluation strategies for learning in the arts

8. Designing curricula in which artists and the resources of arts organizations are effectively used to achieve learning objectives

9. Providing sufficient arts education funding in education budgets and in arts budgets to support the above aims

Wherever those goals have been substantially reached, achievement has been characterized by the development of comprehensive collaborations and partnerships. For instance, in Kansas City, the Kansas City Trusts and Foundations has initiated the ARTS PARTNERS program. Through this innovative project, leading Kansas City arts institutions and four local school systems have joined forces with an arts-in-education service organization to design and coordinate arts activities for grades K-12, designating the appropriate grade level and timing for each arts service throughout the city.

A notable example at the state level is under way in Minnesota, where the state arts agency, state department of education and state alliance for arts education have jointly established and funded the Comprehensive Arts Planning Program (CAPP). This partnership has fundamentally reshaped the arts curriculum and provided for the coordinated use of community resources to assist school systems throughout the state.

Recent examples at the national level include the development of several joint policy statements, including the "Philadelphia Resolution," drafted in 1986 by representatives of 30 arts and education groups, and the paper "Concepts for Strengthening Arts Education in Schools K-12," both products of a series of meetings sponsored by the American Council for the Arts (ACA) and the Music Educators National Conference (MENC).

These examples at the local, state and national levels reflect the authors' knowledge of particular partnerships; other examples would serve equally well in conveying the broad range of alternatives currently being developed by practitioners in the field.

RECOGNIZING THE BASES FOR COLLABORATIONS

The potential for significant collaboration among arts and education organizations can soon be realized, for the following reasons:

1. Representative national arts and education organizations have identified goals for establishing greater communication and initiating more effective collaborations. These organizations include representatives of teachers of the arts (Music Educators National Conference, National Arts Education Association, National Dance Association), the state arts agencies (National Assembly of State Arts Agencies), educators of teachers of the arts (National Associations of Schools of Music, Art and Design, Theatre, and Dance), state legislators (National Council of State Legislators) and arts-in-education service organizations (Young Audiences, American Alliance for Theatre and Education). Furthermore, these national organizations and others are informing their leaders and members of these issues and goals, the benefits of cooperation and how to collaborate effectively.

2. Forums exist for communication. These include ACA's ongoing roundtable and such ad hoc committees as those convened by the National Endowment for the Arts.

3. Public and private grant-making agencies in the arts at the federal, state and local levels are funding collaborations among the arts and education communities. For example, the National Endowment for the Arts has a new category, Arts in States Basic Education Grants, which supports cooperative planning between state arts agencies and state departments of education. Of applications from 42 states, 16 grants were awarded. In addition, state arts agencies and private arts-in-education organizations are expanding the number and increasing the length of artist residencies, as well as broadening the range of their activities to include more statewide conferences on arts and education, curriculum design projects, materials development, teacher inservice training and student evaluation/testing.

4. Examples of planned and spontaneous partnerships abound at the local level, although few communities have achieved the kind of comprehensive partnership noted above in Kansas City.

Because educational decision making is so much a local process, a primary goal of communication and cooperation at the national level should be to replicate recent policy-making forums at the state and local levels. National organizations representing arts and education interests should facilitate communication and collaboration between and within each of the four categories of organizations mentioned earlier—education systems, arts-in-education organizations, resources, and university and professional training organizations. These organizations should be helped to establish working relationships crossing narrow constituency boundaries. Collaboration within each category at the national, state and local levels will help to ensure that goals agreed upon nationally are implemented locally, and that local practice is perceived and acted upon at state and national levels.

Representative organizations should make use of the full range of communication tools at their disposal. These include forums for policy discussion and information exchange as well as policy forums on special topics; joint policy statements; joint setting of research agendas; newsletters and column space in regular and special publications; conferences and regular presentations to one another's leadership; and collaborative advocacy efforts.

A major challenge to the arts and arts education constituency at present is whether they can unite at the local level to advocate the arts as an essential part of basic education. When facing unusually complex problems, politicians are fond of saying, ''What we need is a Marshall Plan,'' referring to the comprehensive plan put together at the end of World War II to revitalize the economies of U.S. allies in Western Europe. What they often fail to note is that the task of conceptualizing and implementing such a mammoth undertaking requires a unity of purpose often lacking among the most vocal supporters of such a plan. Achieving this consensus has proved particularly elusive in the arts education field, despite the best efforts of the most committed theoreticians and practitioners.

The following questions, addressed to those in the field of arts education, are intended to provide a point of departure for discussion.

1. What important goal or objective could be achieved by a collaboration between the arts and education communities

in your locality that could not be achieved by either separately?

2. Are you familiar with good models of collaboration and partnership among arts and educational groups? What made them work? How can they be extended to involve other organizations in the arts and education communities?

3. What role can the organization, agency or institution you represent play in establishing an arts and education partnership in your community?

In a pluralistic society, every community is unique. Each community must have a different set of conditions in place before the goals and aspirations of any segment within that community can be achieved. On a national scale, this "critical mass" can be attained only incrementally: organization by organization, community by community, until finally sufficient progress is made to induce a chain reaction of support throughout the country.

Stephen Kaagan and Sarah Chapman

ADOPTING STRATEGIES FOR ADVOCACY AND ACTION IN ARTS EDUCATION

One of the primary aims of the Interlochen Symposium is to transmit the enthusiasm for action in arts education now felt at state and federal levels to the local level.

For those determined to promote arts education locally, integrating it successfully into school programming, three issues are critical. The first issues is the matter of deciding what is meant by "local." Is the local school district the appropriate unit for cultivating arts education—and, if so, in all instances or only in some? How does one decide on the most appropriate size of the locality for breaking new ground in arts education? The second issue is the matter of finding and nurturing appropriate local champions for arts education. Who might they be? Are there untapped sources of advocacy? What conditions should characterize their individual contributions and their work together as creators, formulators and activators? The third issue is the matter of dramatizing the need for arts education. What are the traditional tools for advocacy? Are they convincing, productive? Can less traditional tools be identified and used to greater effect?

DEFINING THE LOCALITY

The determination of what is meant by "local" may be the most consequential strategy for strengthening arts education on other than federal and state levels. Much of what can be accomplished in arts education is linked to planners' assumptions about tillable ground—the size of a geographic area, populations served, diversity of populations included in programming, capacity of service providers, and the cultural and educational infrastructure within a given area.

The local school district as a unit is only a beginning point for decision making about what constitutes a locality. There are more than 15,000 school districts in the United States. They range in size from Maidstone, Vermont, with no schools, 5 or so students and an annual budget of $13,000 to New York City, with several hundred schools, 900,000 students, and a budget in the millions. Of these districts 80 percent serve 20 percent of the students, and thus 20 percent of the districts serve 80 percent of the students. For this reason, it is almost nonsensical to conclude that the local school district is necessarily the natural unit for fostering arts education.

Although the local school district may not be local for the purposes set forth at the Interlochen Symposium, the local school or school site may be. The school, most would agree, is a potential focal point of enthusiasm, action and programming for arts education—an integral, though not the sole, part of the natural unit. Throughout American history the school itself has served as a locus of cultural development. Local, were it to be defined in Interlochen's terms in 1887, may have fit the template of local school community. The cultural landscape of the United States, however, has been considerably altered since 1887; many museums, universities, galleries, businesses, libraries and theaters that did not exist one hundred years ago have become the centers of cultural development.

The effect of these nonschool institutions collectively is to make the definition of local, as applied to arts education, a judgment call. For example, in northern New England, local arts education might be centered in the array of small school districts along the Connecticut River in Vermont and New Hampshire within easy commuting distance of the Hopkins Center of Dartmouth College. A major cultural facility in the area, Hopkins Center is bringing a version of the heralded Lincoln Center Institutes to parts of two rural states. In western Kansas local arts education may be centered in a block of local districts sustained by a statewide, university-based consortium of organizations. In New York City local may be no bigger than the local elementary school or the community school district.

Accepting a flexible definition of local means that achieving uniform coverage of many states' geographical areas will be extremely difficult. Once "localities" have been defined along strategic lines, there will emerge shaded and unshaded areas. Some parts of a state will not be slated for arts education activity. The danger, of course, is that the areas without arts education may contain populations that might benefit the most from aggressive promotion of arts education. The upside of a flexible definition of local may be its practicability, but the downside may be its unfairness. Planners must be most exacting on the intricate issue of determining the locus for promoting arts education if their work is to be judged astute and if arts education experiences of quality are to be made equally available to all young people.

It seems apparent, then, that "local" may designate an environmental condition, even a state of mind among a cluster of people, as much as it describes a geographic or demographic configuration. Regardless of configuration, however, the locality must have leadership at its center.

It is generally assumed, indeed expected, that leadership originates from school district personnel, from those in positions to lead. But how many members of school boards have in their own lives experienced the arts within a framework of history, criticism, aesthetics and production? How many principals, most of whom are former teachers, have been educated in the arts and have worked to ensure that all children have access to the arts as an essential component of education, on a par with the three Rs? If the majority of parents are also products of arts-deprived educations, to what degree can they be expected to prod or encourage educational leadership toward the inclusion of the arts in a fundamental way? Very little.

SEEKING NEW CHAMPIONS

Can the term "local" perhaps identify a cluster of interested persons, brought together by their shared desire for action, an advocacy unit or a team comprising artists who primarily produce art and artists who teach the arts? If there is agreement that art belongs to everyone, that it contributes to the lives of all people, that it has a history, a content and an aesthetic, then do not the parent, the news reporter, the school principal, the merchant and the art patron each and all have a vital role to play in deepening and nurturing the arts within public and private education? And if art makes a unique contribution to the development of critical thinking, if it is a catalyst for problem solving, if it touches the creative side of every individual, then ought not the scientist, the medical professional and the counselor be equally interested in the integration of the arts into the society through education?

Art is about the individual. Individuals are the merchants, community leaders, principals, school board members, parents. And individuals are the teachers of the arts. Cannot persons be identified within professional, social, cultural, educational and administrative communities to brainstorm, to provoke, to awaken in-

terest in the arts and, in turn, to demand from educational and
political decision makers a more committed policy toward the inclusion of the arts within education?

Are there not parents, grandparents, citizens throughout communities who have had intensive private study or hold university
degrees in the arts, persons who have had few opportunities to
share their knowledge with others? Might not the schools invite
these persons to contribute to their programs through guest lec-
tures, exhibits, performances, teaching? Perhaps a lecturer on one
topic would spend two weeks traveling from one classroom to the
next, from one school to another, giving the same lecture. Are
there not persons in the community who create macrame, paint
watercolors, sketch portraits, read poetry, write short stories,
know the history of a Chopin waltz—who could be invited to
share that knowledge of the arts with students on a weekly basis,
not just once a year at an arts festival?

Might not the community playhouse present a repeat performance of the senior class play, so that audiences would be expanded
to include not only the school population and parents but a larger
public, and so that the students might interact with the community actors, with the playhouse personnel and with one another in
that context?

A good example of how the energy of new champions can coa-
lesce into a successful effort is Project HEART, an acronym for
Helping Education through Arts Resources for Teachers, which is
located in the Decatur and Champaign, Illinois school districts.
Economic decline had resulted in the elimination of the elementary
art-specialist position, thus endangering the art program. A community leader gathered a group of art advocates from businesses,
universities, schools and service organizations. She secured federal
funds to develop a teacher-support program, based on experiences
in the history, criticism and production of art and architecture—all
at minimal cost to the school district. The school administrators re-
sponded enthusiastically to the workshops and endorsed implementation of a model program in a magnet school. Within a
relatively short time, the tide turned. Instead of eliminating an art
program the community was generating ideas for how to continue
it in a multifaceted context, with funding secured from sources external to school district budgets.

FINDING NEW TOOLS

As new advocates come together in more organically defined geographic regions to promote arts education, they will need new
tools. Existing ones will have to be reshaped and augmented;
novel components will have to be added. Eloquent philosophizing
on how the arts sensitize and acculturate young people will not be
enough in an era of broadened arts education advocacy. Nor will it
be sufficient to demonstrate through exemplary projects how the
arts excite the enthusiasm and stimulate the creativity of the students they serve. Neither of these strategies must be abandoned.
They have been the mainstay of arts education advocates. But others should be added as fortification for the tough battles ahead, at
quarters closer to local school governance.

   A central element in a strategy of advocating anything is to tell
those you are trying to convince what the aim is and why it is so
important to their welfare. The trouble with most arguments for
arts education is not that they lack inherent validity—they have
that—but that they are seldom related to the concerns of the audience. Most arguments for arts education focus primarily and often
exclusively on quality-of-life goals, neglecting almost totally the
implications for our culture and students' employment opportunities, which are concerns of major constituents. The focal points for
a cogent statement on behalf of arts education should be the implications of artistic study for (1) the employment of graduating students; (2) a culture increasingly dominated by visual images; and
(3) as part of the requisites of a desirable quality of life, including
both performances and appreciation of the arts. What is suggested, in effect, is for arts advocates to fashion their case as much
on instrumentality as on inherent worth.

   In addition to being tailored to particular audiences, almost
every successful case statement includes data. Arts education, like
other endeavors, will be unable to escape these necessary evils.
''The power of the bottom line,'' or hard statistical data, has yet to
be generally tested in advocacy for arts education. Potential advocates inexperienced in handling quantifiable research may be
alarmed, but the potential contribution of data to advocacy issues
must be acknowledged. The object is to develop a set of indicators
or data points that will tell a story about the role of the arts in the
educational process. The list that follows offers indicators that
might be charted. (None of the indicators are student performance measures, the traditional stumbling block to reporting
the arts.)

1. Number of jobs in the Department of Labor dictionary of occupations that require or might be stimulated by arts education, comparing figures for 1965 and the present

2. Number of local districts that require fine arts experience for graduation

3. Number of colleges that require arts experience for admission

4. Number of Advanced Placement Arts programs in high schools and number of enrollees

5. Quantitative correlation of arts interests with high school retention

6. Quantitative results from an inventory of partnerships between schools and cultural institutions.

The point here is not to provide a definitive list of the most desirable data elements but rather to urge courage in developing one, collecting the data and promulgating the results.

For good or ill, society wants to keep score. On some of the most important aspects of life it may not be possible to do so, but success in the public forum is directly related to a willingness to subject goals and achievements to quantitative analysis, however seemingly unjust at times. To advocate means to "speak to"—to speak to someone is assumed. And those "someones" increasingly insist on receiving information that has been analyzed and evaluated. To provide less than that is unacceptable.

SHAPING A STRATEGY

The strategy begins with a release from previously held notions of the meaning of local. Advocates must seek release from employing traditional networks, from relying on the same set of doers to make the same pleas for attention and dollars. To seek new directions involves risk. Not to do so also involves risk—that outdated structures, ineffective organizations and antiquated approaches will continue to shape the present and control the future. Advocates must begin to analyze the actual boundaries and identify their potential allies.

It is incumbent upon advocates of arts education to insist that those who promote educational reform reach the sources of decision making and implementation within the community, of which the schools are a significant part. Those who have been appointed or elected to positions of educational and political leadership must be held accountable for providing the best possible education for all students. They simply are not doing their jobs if they fail to create new avenues, seek alternative structures and reach out toward untapped resources within the schools and throughout the community. The advocates of arts education fail also if they do not insist on dialogue; "more of the same" will not suffice. They must energetically commit themselves to challenging a larger political audience to examine the status of arts education in their particular locality and to generate enthusiasm for rethinking the barriers and boundaries of action, reaction and interaction.

Advocates must discover ways to convert the information pouring forth from national levels in arts education into arguments, including data, that will be convincing in localities. They must use both research and anecdotes as tools for tilling new soil. They must rediscover their personal resources and ignite the energies of neighbors and colleagues. In so doing, they can begin to foster growth, gradual though it may be, until the people most immediately affected by legislative and educational reform will be the same people who advocated that the arts play a prominent part in that reform.

For those who will be shaping these new strategies, the vision of where one hopes to arrive will largely dictate how to begin. It will be essential to analyze the immediate environment, develop strategies for securing additional resources as needed and implement ideas in realistic stages.

It will also be necessary to acknowledge the creative energies represented by the interested, action-oriented groups who step forward to share in the vision, as these groups can provide invaluable guidance for initial administration and longer term leadership.

To introduce a greater sense of reality and a keener sense of practicality from the start, it is important to assess the degree to which formerly generated ideas and former programs will be built upon or diminished. Any blueprint for action should include attention to those changes.

Finally, it is important to decide on the degree of championship that can be undertaken and maintained. That decision will help shape the initial plans, affect the schedules established for moving forward and attract a like-minded group of persons to the endeavor. The initial questions to be explored include deciding how to define the local community and what degree of change is desired; deciding how to account for as many students as possible, while reviewing and perhaps revising specific allocations of resources; deciding how to identify potential champions, capture

their interest, sustain their energies and support their advocacy;
balancing the goals of arts champions and artists and arts educators; deciding how to gather the necessary data to inform and persuade your adversaries and how to find release from old ways of
advocacy and to adopt new ways of pressing the case for arts education so that it is nurtured at the local level.

3
The Proposals

DISCUSSION GROUP RECOMMENDATIONS

Group 1

1. Education must focus on the life of the individual school and the children therein. Each child deserves the opportunity to develop all dimensions of his or her person. Each child deserves the opportunity to explore a diversity of subjects and fields.

To achieve these goals, arts educators must collaborate with a broad range of colleagues in the arts, humanities, and sciences in developing a school agenda which improves the total life of the school and allows each child to reach his or her full potential. This means that the Interlochen Symposium's compelling case for improving the state of arts education must ultimately translate to our participation in an overall effort to improve education in the schools.

2. Be it resolved that we support the following specifics:

   A. Every junior and senior high school should have at least seven instructional periods per day.

   B. Approximately 15 percent of the instructional program of every student at every level, K-12, should be devoted to the arts.

   C. Every high school should require at least two units of study in music, art, theater, or dance for graduation.

   D. Every college or university should require at least one course in music, art, theater, or dance for admission and one course in the arts for graduation.

   E. Every prospective elementary classroom teacher should have at least 12 semester hours of credit in methods and materials for teaching the arts.

   F. Every school district should employ qualified supervisors in the visual and performing arts.

3. The Ad Hoc National Arts Education Working Group should expand the signers of the "Philadelphia Resolution" and the "Concepts for Strengthening Arts Education in Schools" documents and should develop strategies for implementing action items that might grow out of this conference; and strategies from the "Philadelphia Resolution" and the "Concepts" documents and the Interlochen Symposium should be placed on the agendas of the national associations during 1988 for endorsement.

Group 2

1. We recommend that a national group assume responsibility to serve as spokesperson at the national level for the arts in education. Further—and of primary importance—we recommend that this group create a coalition of representatives from the professional arts education community to serve as coordinating council to ensure ongoing dialogue and accurate representation of priorities, topical issues, and areas of concern to arts educators throughout the United States.

2. We recommend that a national group create a five-year long-range plan to capture the public's imagination regarding the import and impact of arts education in the United States. A partial list of items for this plan includes:

   A. Development and dissemination of planning instruments for use at the local level to stimulate support for arts education.

   B. Collection of all significant materials related to arts education—including advocacy and strategy models, curriculum materials, and development of arts-related issues—to be housed and disseminated from a central library.

3. We recommend that a national group convene symposia at the national level for non-arts constituents (National School Boards Association, Council of Chief State School Officers, National Governors' Association, National Conference of Mayors, American Association of School Administrators, etc.) to inform them of the important role of the arts in education and to generate among their ranks support for the arts as basic to the school curriculum.

Group 3

1. The Ad Hoc National Arts Education Working Group supports
    the concept of arts education every day for all students.

2. As participants in the Interlochen Symposium, we endorse the
    "Philadelphia Resolution" and "Concepts for Strengthening
    Arts Education in Schools" developed by the Ad Hoc National
    Arts Education Working Group. These statements should be
    distributed nationally. A systematic effort is needed to place the
    resolution on the agenda of major organizational meetings and
    conferences dealing with the arts in education. Public service
    announcements and other communications should be devel-
    oped urging the adoption and implementation of the "Philadel-
    phia Resolution." A national group should also plan and
    develop inservice staff development programs aimed at specific
    themes of the resolution and the outcome of this symposium.

3. A national group should serve as an informational resource:

    A. We should work to develop a data base for the arts in edu-
        cation, with categories that are appropriate to the needs of
        groups seeking to collaborate and network with others.

    B. We should initiate a historical review and analysis of collab-
        orative efforts in the arts *and* in other fields to provide guid-
        ance to individuals and groups.

    C. We should develop models of individual and/or group col-
        laboration that give emphasis to the diverse resources and
        patterns that are possible. We should document strategies
        for various arts groups to network.

    D. We should strive to achieve a unified focus for the arts in
        education at a national level.

Group 4

1. A single conceptual approach to curriculum development is rec-
    ommended. It should include instruction in the following con-
    tent areas: A) production and performance; B) analysis,
    interpretation and evaluation; and C) historical and cultural
    knowledge. This approach must be taken with regard to all five
    disciplines, or art forms, if you wish, including creative writing.
    This conceptual approach permits multiple applications through
    curricula and will require teacher education programs to pro-

vide new courses that enable teachers to translate this content to children at different age levels.

2. A handbook should be developed that provides direction for effective collaborations based on successful models.

3. We charge the Ad Hoc National Arts Education Working Group to address the need for a national organization to serve as umbrella spokesman for arts education.

4. There needs to be a national enclave of champions consisting of the CEOs of major corporations who will advocate arts education.

5. A glossary is needed to define the terminology of arts education.

Group 5

1. The Ad Hoc National Arts Education Working Group should broaden the scope of this arts education coalition, at the national level, to include the organized groups of artists and educators, including, for example, the Screen Actors' Guild, the American Federation of Teachers, and industries which benefit from arts education.

2. The American Council for the Arts should be encouraged to continue expanding and intensifying its interest in arts education by such means as disseminating information about model arts education projects and collaborative efforts among arts agencies, and reporting on the findings of the two Arts Education Research Centers, at New York University and the University of Illinois, funded by the National Endowment for the Arts.

3. The Ad Hoc National Arts Education Working Group should be encouraged to facilitate the dissemination of existing national standards and guidelines for each arts discipline.

Group 6

1. All members of society should be knowledgeably interactive in all art forms. A variety of levels of involvement and achievement in the arts are appropriate, but K-12 education must provide the means to this general end.

2. This goal can only be achieved through effective partnerships, which we define as *formal* agreements into which parties delib-

erately enter and for which they are accountable. Partnerships must be founded upon mutual understanding and respect, they must include all key stakeholders, and they must include agreements on outcomes.

3. Therefore, let us form a partnership. Let us agree that all participants in this conference will now move to broaden the base of endorsement for the "Philadelphia Resolution" and the "Concepts for Strengthening Arts Education in Schools," both within their own organizations and beyond. Questions raised should be returned to a core group for consideration and potential revisions to the statements. Expansion of the dialogue is a key objective. This process, in itself, is the beginning of action toward the stated goals. We must also designate an accountable party who is charged to track and shepherd the process.

Group 7

1. We recommend that a national policy consortium on arts education be established, with representation from:
   - professional arts education associations,
   - arts providers,
   - arts advocacy groups, and
   - government agencies.

The purposes of the consortium would be:
   - to set an agenda for arts education policy and longitudinal research; and
   - to coordinate national advocacy efforts, including the development of a White House conference on arts education.

2. We recommend that those forming arts education partnerships act on the following:
   - identify the pool of potential partners and constituents;
   - address articulated needs recognizing the essential role of teachers at every level of decision making;
   - set a common agenda;
   - identify ongoing roles for partners;
   - maintain open communication about the individual agendas and resources of partners; and
   - see that the partnerships have a continuing impact on arts education.

3. We recommend that we broaden the recognition of stakeholders in arts education to include:

- elected government officials and appointed policy makers at all levels,
- trade unions,
- arts education researchers,
- arts-related industries,
- print and broadcast media, and
- constituencies which demographic change is bringing to the fore, such as older Americans, multi-cultural populations and new generations of artists and teachers.

Group 8

We recommend:

1. That the list of key players to be involved in partnerships at the local level be expanded from artists, teachers, and scholars to include chief school district administrators, building principals, parents and students, where appropriate.

2. That the arts education field take concerted affirmative action by listing its accomplishments and growth of activity over the last one or two decades and that the field establish a national network for:

   A. policy, political action and advocacy
   B. technical assistance to the field by experienced field practitioners (hook up people doing it, with the solutions, to people asking the questions and seeking help)
   C. the research and capturing of data which provide evidence of growth
   D. ideas and strategies regarding the institutionalization of the idea/concept

3. That the arts education field declare an armistice or moratorium on internecine warfare and consider the following list of what we have identified as obstacles to concerted action and effective advocacy at the national, state, and local levels. We further recommend that this list serve as an action agenda for the field in its search for solutions to some of the problems that have plagued the field for years and stood in the way of progress.

List of Obstacles to Concerted Action and Effective Advocacy for Arts Education at the National, State, and Local Levels

- Communication/lack of common vocabulary
- Unwillingness to understand other person's point of view
- Professional and personal pride, jealousy, and fear of invasion/ erosion of power or "turf"
- No clear definition of territory and responsibility
- Personal and professional insecurity
- Lack of knowledge of how to connect with other like-minded advocates
- Inability to know when to compromise and that compromise is not tantamount to losing face; how to create win-win situations; fear of losing credit or taking blame
- Classroom teachers and artists in schools as arts specialists
- Don't know to whom, when, where, and how to "advocate"
- Lack of interest in the fields or narrow-mindedness about them
- Lack of an appropriate, creditable forum in which to discuss an action/advocacy agenda or plan
- Lack of a common value or priority system
- Lack of extrinsic, tangible rewards—financial, public awareness, government
- Different and often conflicting criteria and methodology
- Lack of accessible basic research
- Only one right way of doing it
- Entrenched personal and political history—won't change the way we do it
- No commonly accepted definition, let alone term, for arts in education; no agreement on who teaches what to whom, how, when, and where; disagreement on who should pay for it
- Current inflexible structure and operation of most schools/systems
- Too narrow a definition of arts (what's considered "art" and "education")
- Lack of a national policy that reflects all of the divergence within the field and insufficient, narrowly-based federal leadership and vision

Group 9

1. We need to develop a unified voice on both the national and local levels responsible for pursuing arts education goals and for implementing the strategy described in Stephen Kaagan and Sarah Chapman's paper *Advocacy and Action: Strategies for*

Strengthening Arts Education. This voice should be representative of a coalition that includes the groups here at Interlochen, plus other groups not present, such as museums and cultural institutions, unions, artists, arts scholars (historians, etc.), and K-12 arts specialists.
On the local level, structures will need to be identified or invented to provide a unified voice on those *levels.* For extending this coalition, it is essential to be more inclusive of the ethnic diversity of the country.

2. Our group values a comprehensive pattern of collaborations and recognizes that a successful partnership requires constant collaboration on three levels:

   A. Planning which involves all partners and includes setting clear goals and assuring that artists, arts resource people, and educators understand each other's expectations and limitations;
   B. Working together in the same time and place throughout the project;
   C. Follow-up both by teachers and arts resource people.

3. New models do exist which demonstrate and prove that collaborations with multiple partners can expand the financial support to arts education and transcend apparent problems of competition for limited funds and that the growth of partnerships does not supplant teacher specialists but instead has stimulated the rehiring of teachers.

Group 10

1. *Instructional Components*

   K-12 arts instruction should include visual arts, music, dance, drama, and writing. The instructional components should address:

   A. production/creation and performance
   B. analysis, interpretation, and evaluation
   C. historical and cultural understandings

   Curriculum should be defined by local participation, utilizing arts specialists, teachers, artists, administrators, and community resources, and it should reflect multi-cultural concerns and values. Evaluation strategies should emerge from the nature of the individual art forms and the concerns of the instructional components.

2. *Partnerships*

We recommend that participants in arts education aim for more than just parity with other education disciplines. Rather, we should take advantage of the leadership and resources offered by partnerships and collaborations among those in education and the arts—to help students reach their full potential in every aspect of learning.

3. *Advocacy*

It is recommended that a national group be encouraged to continue providing leadership in bringing together arts education leaders from both the arts and the education communities at the national, regional, state, and local levels; and that a national coalition be formed to develop a "how-to" manual to be used in arts education advocacy with school boards and other public officials.

NOTE: Where specific recommendations named American Council for the Arts, Music Educators National Conference, or ACA and MENC together, the wording has been changed to "a national group." Discussion of the composition of this group will be undertaken by the Ad Hoc National Arts Education Working Group.

THE INTERLOCHEN PROPOSAL

November 8, 1987

The one hundred and fifty delegates to the Interlochen Symposium, comprising representatives of the fields of education, arts, and arts education, believe that:

WHEREAS education must focus on the child, how the child learns and interacts in the school environment; and

WHEREAS each child deserves the opportunity to develop all dimensions of his or her being; and

WHEREAS each child should have the opportunity to explore a diversity of subjects and fields:

THEREFORE, to achieve these goals, arts educators must collaborate with a broad range of colleagues in the arts, humanities, and sciences to develop a school agenda that improves the total life of the school and allows each child to reach his or her full potential. We must participate in an overall effort to improve education in the schools.

WHEREAS all members of society should be knowledgeable and interactive in all art forms; and

WHEREAS a variety of levels of involvement and achievement in the arts are appropriate:

THEREFORE, American schools, K-12, should provide arts education for all students every day. Instruction in the arts should encompass visual arts, music, dance, theater, and creative writing. It should be accorded resources of time, money, and personnel equivalent to other basic subject areas, and the same level of expertise. Every school should have an in-school sequential arts program that serves all the children.

To accomplish these fundamental goals for arts education, we endorse the following:

1. We recommend that all participants in this conference will now move to broaden the base of endorsement for the "Philadelphia Resolution" and the "Concepts for Strengthening Arts Education in the Schools," both in their own organizations and beyond. Questions raised should be returned to a core group for consideration and potential revisions of the statements. Expansion of the dialogue is a key objective.

2. We recommend that the need for a national organization to serve as umbrella spokesman for arts education be addressed. Among the purposes to be served by such a body would be the following:
   - formulation of a five-year plan for expansion of arts education
   - conducting national symposia on arts education for non-arts education constituents
   - providing leadership in bringing together arts education leaders at national, state, and local levels

3. We recommend recognition of the following groups or stakeholders in arts education, and we recommend efforts to include these groups in the coalition working for arts education:
   - professional arts education associations
   - museums and cultural institutions
   - arts providers and arts producing organizations
   - elected government officials
   - appointed policy-workers
   - artist unions
   - teacher unions
   - service organizations of educational administrators
   - arts education researchers
   - arts related industries
   - print and broadcast media
   - arts advocacy groups
   - government arts agencies
   - colleagues in the humanities
   - colleagues in the sciences
   - constituencies becoming more influential as demographics change, including multi-cultural populations and older Americans
   - special populations
   - parent and student populations
   - artists

4. We recommend the development of informational resources, including:
- a data base concerning activities and programs in arts
education
- a historical analysis of collaborative efforts in the arts
- an analysis of models of individual and group collaboration an arts education
- a glossary which defines the terminology of arts
education
- a compendium of national standards and guidelines for
individual arts

5. We recommend:
- the inclusion of production/creation and performance,
analysis and evaluation, and historical and cultural understandings in instructional programs in the arts
- that the content of instructional programs in the arts be
developed by the specialist teachers in consultation
with artists, administrators, and other knowledgeable
persons in the community
- that the content of instructional programs in the arts reflect multi-cultural concerns and values
- that strategies be developed for evaluation that addresses the nature of the individual art forms and their
respective instructional components

6. We recommend the following conditions in schools and
colleges:
- that every secondary school have at least seven periods
a day, a length sufficient to permit study of the arts
- that approximately 15 percent of the instructional program of every student at all levels, K-12, be devoted to
the arts
- that every high school require at least two units of
study in music, art, theater, dance and creative writing
for graduation
- that every college or university require at least one
course in music, theater, art, or dance for admission,
and one course in these disciplines for graduation
- that every prospective classroom teacher have at least
12 semester hours of credit in methods and materials
for teaching the arts
- that every school district employ qualified supervisors
in the visual and performing arts

Appendix

THE STEERING COMMITTEE

Richard F. Bell is the national program director of Young Audiences, Inc., and executive and artistic director of The Theatre Institute at Storm King. He was producing artistic director at the American Kaleidoscope Theatre and has taught at the State University of New York at New Paltz, Hamilton College, and Columbia University School of the Arts. He has served as an advisor for Opera America's Repertory Directory of Children's Opera and as a member of the Grants Review Panel for the Westchester Arts Council and of the Ad Hoc National Arts Education Working Group. He is the author of *Young Audiences Program Booklets: A Guide for Performing Artists*.

Sarah A. Chapman is chairperson and professor in the Department of Dance at Temple University. She has worked as a consultant in children's dance throughout the East Coast and has served on an ad hoc advocacy committee for public policy K-12 document. She is a is past-president of the Pennsylvania State Dance Association and is a member of the Pennsylvania State Aesthetic Arts Education curriculum planning task force. She has contributed to the following publications: *The History of Dance in Art and Education* (1979), *Try a New Face* (1977), and *Movement Education in the U.S.* (1973).

Charles Dorn is chairman and professor in the Department of Art Education at Florida State University. He is a past-president of the National Art Education Association (NAEA) and a former head of the Department of Art at California State University. He has directed an international leadership conference in art education in Belgrade, Yugoslavia and a 1977 NAEA commission on art education. He is the recipient of the Twenty-Fifth Anniversary Award for Distinguished Service to Education in Art from the National Gallery of Art and of the NAEA Distinguished Service Award. He authored the *Project IMPACT* proposal for U.S. Office of Education and the Contract for Involvement of Professional Education Associations Retraining of Personnel to Engage in Career Education in 1978. Among his published work are numerous articles in *Art Education*; chapters for *The NAEA Bicentennial Commission Report, The Curriculum Handbook for School Administrators* (AASA) and *The Artist/Teacher Institute Report*; and *Artists Teachers Perspective* publications for NAEA.

Robert Glidden   is a professor of music and dean of the School of
Music at Florida State University. He is a past-president of Pi Kappa
Lambda National Music Honor Society and has been president, vice president, and treasurer of the National Association of Schools of Music. He
was vice president of the American Council for the Arts in Education. He
served on the National Endowment for the Arts' Task Force on the Education, Training and Development of Artists and Arts Educators and
chaired the Advanced Placement Music Committee. He has published various articles on music administration in higher education and on accreditation.

Lonna Jones   is a program associate for special projects at the Rockefeller Brothers Fund, where she previously served as director for awards
in arts education. She has also worked with the United States Department
of Education as a policy analyst and manager, as a grants officer in the
Special Concerns Division, as special assistant to the United States Commissioner of Education, and as a specialist in private-public relations. She
was staff assistant to the director of the President's Commission on Instructional Technology (1968-1970), which produced a report entitled *To
Improve Learning*. She has had articles and essays published in *Horizon,
Design, Daedalus, High Fidelity/Musical America* and *American Education*
magazines. She is co-author of *Research in Arts Education: A Federal Chapter*
published by the U.S. Government Printing Office.

Stephen S. Kaagan   is commissioner of education in the state of Vermont. He has served as provost at Pratt Institute, Brooklyn, New York, as
deputy commissioner and director of planning and policy development
for the Massachusetts Department of Education, and as a special assistant
to the United States Deputy Commissioner of Education for Development.
He has been published in several magazines and journals, including *Educational Leadership, Educational Planning,* and *American Personnel Journal*. He
has authored ''Assessment and Evaluation of Education in the United
States,'' a position statement of the Council of Chief State School Officers, and ''Strengthening the State's Role in Supporting the Individual
Artist,'' a study commissioned by the Massachusetts Council on the Arts
and Humanities.

Jonathan Katz   is executive director of the National Assembly of State
Arts Agencies (NASAA). He is a former professor of arts administration
and director of the Community Arts Management Program at Sangamon
State University in Springfield, Illinois. He has served as executive director of The Children's Museum of Denver and as executive director of the

Kansas Arts Commission. He co-edited *Consumer Behavior and the Arts*, a special issue of *The Journal of Arts Management and the Law* and is the editor of *The Arts and Education Handbook: Issues and Opportunities* and *A Quick and Easy Guide to Demographic Information*, both for published by NASAA.

Paul R. Lehman is professor and associate dean, School of Music, at the University of Michigan, Ann Arbor. He has been a professional music educator since 1953. He is a past-president of Music Educators National Conference served as a music specialist with the United States Office of Education. He has been a conductor, performer, author, clinician, and adjudicator and is the author of more than 100 articles, reviews, and books about music education and arts education.

Kathryn A. Martin is dean at the School of Fine and Performing Arts, Wayne State University. She has served as president of the International Council of Fine Arts Deans, and she is a member of the Michigan Council for the Arts, a founding member of the Great Lakes Arts Alliance, and a member of the National Program Committee for Young Audiences, Inc. She has written articles for *Design, Teachers in the Arts*, and *Educational Digest* and was executive editor of *Theatre Resource Handbook/ Directory*, published by the National Endowment for the Arts.

Jerrold Ross is associate dean for academic affairs at New York University's School of Education, Health, Nursing and Arts Professions. He is a trustee and past-president of the Usdan Center for the Creative and Performing Arts. He has been chairman of the Teacher Education Department and president of the New York College of Music, a council member for the College Music Society, a member of the Graduate Commission for the National Association of Schools of Music, and a consultant for the New Jersey Department of Higher Education. He has published articles in *Design for Arts in Education, Journal of Proceedings* (National Association of Schools of Music), *Horizon*, and *Journal of the Council for Research in Music Education*.

Thomas A. Shannon has practiced law both in the private sector and as a schools attorney. He has served as deputy superintendent for administration for San Diego City Schools and is currently executive director of the National School Boards Association. He is executive publisher of *American School Board Journal*.

Richard Sinatra is professor and chairperson of Human Services and Counseling at St. John's University. He was elected chairperson of Arts in Education Network of the Association for Supervision and Curriculum Development in 1985, and he has been an English teacher, reading specialist, district reading coordinator, university professor in graduate education, and director of a reading clinic. He has been published in *Roeper Review* and *Early Years*. His books include *Using the Right Brain in the Language Arts* (with J. Stahl-Gemake) and *Visual Literacy Connections to Thinking, Reading, and Writing*.

THE INTERLOCHEN PARTICIPANTS

Andrew Ackerman
New York State Council on the
    Arts
New York, New York

Helen Almanza
Very Special Arts
Washington, D.C.

Dean Amhaus
Duncan and Associates
Washington, D.C.

Susan Ball
College Art Association of
    America
New York, New York

William Banchs
National Foundation for
    Advancement in the Arts
Miami, Florida

Lt. Col. James M. Bankhead
US Air Force Band
Washington, D.C.

Connie Beardsley
National Assembly of Local
    Arts Agencies
Carlsbad, California

Thomas Becker
American Council for the Arts
New York, New York

Roger L. Bedard
American Alliance for Theatre
    and Education
Blacksburg, Virginia

Richard Bell
Young Audiences
New York, New York

Donald Bemis
Utica Community Schools
Utica, Michigan

Jeanne Bluechel
Public Relations and Public
    Affairs
Bellevue, Washington

Janice Blush
Montana Young Audiences
Missoula, Montana

Mary Jane Bolin
Board of Cooperative
    Educational Services
of Nassau County
Westbury, New York

Joan Boyett
Los Angeles Music Center
Los Angeles, California

Jerry D. Bryan
National School Boards
    Association
Tipton, Oklahoma

Bert A. Burda
Idaho State Department of
    Education
Boise, Idaho

Robert Buzbee
The Sears-Roebuck Foundation
Chicago, Illinois

Mary Ann Cameron
Music Educators National
    Conference
Reston, Virginia

Sarah Chapman
National Dance Association
Philadelphia, Pennsylvania

Elizabeth Childs
Minnesota State Arts Boards
St. Paul, Minnesota

Jane Christensen
National Council of Teachers of
    English
Urbana, Illinois

William Cleveland
California Confederation of the
    Arts
Citrus Heights, California

Shirley Contino-Phillips
Council for the Arts in
    Westchester, Inc.
White Plains, New York

Donald L. Corbett
Music Educators National
    Conference
Wichita, Kansas

Shirley Trusty Corey
American Alliance for Theatre
    and Education
New Orleans, Louisiana

Beth Cornell
Performing Tree
Los Angeles, California

Candra Day
Ensemble Theater Company
Mills Alley, California

Lina Dean
Interlochen Center for the Arts
Interlochen, Michigan

Michael Delp
Interlochen Center for the Arts
Interlochen, Michigan

Margaret DiBlasio
American Association of Col-
    leges for Teacher Education
Minneapolis, Minnesota

Charles Dorn
National Art Education
    Association
Tallahassee, Florida

Lani Lattin Duke
Getty Center for Education in
    the Arts
Los Angeles, California

Herbert Ferrer
Michigan Council for the Arts
Detroit, Michigan

Charles Fowler
Musical America
Washington, D.C.

Richard Gage
Illinois Arts Council
Chicago, Illinois

Paul Germaine-Brown
Artists Collective
Hartford, Connecticut

Elissa O. Getto
Richard B. Baumgardner Center
    for the Performing Arts
Clearwater, Florida

Roger Gilmore
National Association of Schools
    of Art and Design
Chicago, Illinois

Drew H. Gitomer
Educational Testing Service
Princeton, New Jersey

Nancy Glaze
David and Lucile Packard
    Foundation
Los Altos, California

Avery L. Glenn
Utah State Office of Education
Salt Lake City, Utah

Karl Glenn
Music Educators National
    Conference
Wayne, Michigan

Robert Glidden
National Association of Schools
    of Music
Tallahassee, Florida

Barbara Goldman
National Assembly of State Arts
    Agencies
Detroit, Michigan

Jack Golodner
AFL-CIO
Washington, D.C.

Gary Goree
Tulsa Public Schools
Tulsa, Oklahoma

David Greene
The College Board
Crawfordsville, Indiana

Beverly Grova
National Assembly of Local
    Arts Agencies
Aptos, California

Jerome Grove
Alliance for Independent
    Colleges of Art
Detroit, Michigan

Barbara Hall
Freelance Writer
Brooklyn, New York

Margie Hanson
National Dance Association
Reston, Virginia

Marie B. Harvey
Wayne State University
Detroit, Michigan

Jerome Hausman
Urban Gateways
Evanston, Illinois

Sarah Havens
American Council for the Arts
New York, New York

Susan Heath
Utah Arts Council
Salt Lake City, Utah

Steve Hedden
University of Arizona
Tucson, Arizona

Deborah Hayman
Alexander Julian, Inc.
New York, New York

Howard Hintze
Interlochen Center for the Arts
Interlochen, Michigan

Wade Hobgood
South Carolina Arts
    Commission
Rock Hill, South Carolina

Charles Hoffer
Music Educators National
    Conference
Gainesville, Florida

Diane Howe
National Dance Association
Irvine, California

Roger Jacobi
Interlochen Center for the Arts
Interlochen, Michigan

Inga Johnson
Idaho Commission on the Arts
Boise, Idaho

Lonna Jones
Rockefeller Brothers Fund
New York, New York

Stephen Kaagan
Vermont Department of
    Education
Montpelier, Vermont

Jonathan Katz
National Assembly of State Arts
    Agencies
Washington, D.C.

Ruth Ann Knapp
Michigan Music Educators
    Association
Saginaw, Michigan

Marcia Knoll
Association for Supervision and
    Curriculum Development
Briarwood, New York

Kathy Lawyer
Illinois Alliance for Arts
    Education
Des Plaines, Illinois

Fred Lazarus IV
Maryland Institute, College of
    Art
Baltimore, Maryland

Paul Lehman
Music Educators National
    Conference
Ann Arbor, Michigan

James Lindstrom
National Education Association
Vadnais Heights, Minnesota

Ronald L. Longstreth
International Thespian Society
Cincinnati, Ohio

Meg Madden
San Francisco Ballet
San Francisco, California

Stanley Madeja
Northern Illinois University
DeKalb, Illinois

John J. Mahlmann
Music Educators National
    Conference
Reston, Virginia

Arthur Mark
Business and Industry for the
    Arts in Education
East Stroudsburg, Pennsylvania

Kathryn A. Martin
International Council of Fine
    Arts Deans
Detroit, Michigan

Kenneth May
South Carolina Arts
    Commission
Columbia, South Carolina

Helvi McClelland
Council for the Arts, MIT
Cambridge, Massachusetts

Margaret McKerrow
National Association of Schools
    of Theatre
San Diego, California

John McLaughlin
American Council for the Arts
New York, New York

Dollie McLean
Artists Collective
Hartford, Connecticut

Charles McWhorter
American Ballet Theater
New York, New York

Chris Menke
Wisconsin Arts Board
Madison, Wisconsin

E. Andrew Mills
State Education Department
Albany, New York

Jack Morrison
Consultant in the Arts
West Hollywood, California

Joan Newberg
California State Summer School
    Arts Foundation
Encino, California

Joseph Orlando
Interlochen Center for the Arts
Interlochen, Michigan

Carol Parssinen
Philadelphia Alliance for
    Teaching Humanities in the
    Schools
Philadelphia, Pennsylvania

Frank Philip
Michigan Department of
    Education
Lansing, Michigan

Richard Pioli
Association for Supervision and
    Curriculum Development
Rockville, Maryland

Elsa Posey
American Dance Guild
Northport, New York

Charles A. Qualley
National Art Education
    Association
Boulder, Colorado

Martin Rayala
Wisconsin Department of Public
    Instruction
Madison, Wisconsin

Jane Remer
Consultant
New York, New York

Milton Rhodes
American Council for the Arts
New York, New York

Karen Rice
Opera America
Washington, D.C.

Berda Rittenhouse
New Jersey Council on the Arts
Trenton, New Jersey

Joyce Robinson
Marie Walsh Sharp Art
    Foundation
Colorado Springs, Colorado

Jerrold Ross
National Center for Research in
    Arts Education
New York, New York

Nadine Saitlin
Illinois Alliance for Arts
    Education Board
Chicago, Illinois

Jerry Samuelson
California State University at
    Fullerton
Fullerton, California

Nancy Brooks Schmitz
Teacher College, Columbia
    University
New York, New York

Thomas A. Shannon
National School Boards
    Association
Alexandria, Virginia

Nancy Larson Shapiro
Teachers & Writers
    Collaborative
New York, New York

Pamela Sharp
San Francisco Education Fund
Palo Alto, California

Richard Sinatra
Association for Supervision and
    Curriculum Development
Sea Cliff, New York

Martin J. Skomal
Nebraska Arts Council
Omaha, Nebraska

Larry Stein
Young Audiences
New York, New York

Chris Stolery
Wisdom Bridge
Chicago, Illinois

Scott Stoner
Alliance for Arts Education
Washington, D.C.

Ann Straus
Young Audiences
New York, New York

John Straus
American Council for the Arts
New York, New York

Bennett Tarleton
National Assembly of State Arts
    Agencies
Nashville, Tennessee

Ronald Teachworth
Utica Public School System
Utica, Michigan

Keith Thompson
National Center for Research in
    Arts Education
Urbana, Illinois

Chris Van Antwerp
Michigan Association of
    Community Arts Agencies
Grand Rapids, Michigan

Roberta Volkman
Illinois State Board of Education
Springfield, Illinois

Robert Werner
National Association of Schools
    of Music
Cincinnati, Ohio

David Willoughby
College Music Society
Portales, New Mexico

Barbara Salisbury Wills
American Alliance for Theatre
    and Education
Austin, Texas

Daniel Windham
New York Philharmonic
New York, New York

Trudy Zimmerman
Learning Through Education in
    the Arts Project
San Francisco, California

ABOUT THE AMERICAN COUNCIL FOR THE ARTS

The American Council for the Arts (ACA) is one of the nation's primary sources of legislative news affecting all of the arts and serves as a leading advisor to arts administrators, educators, elected officials, arts patrons and the general public. To accomplish its goal of strong advocacy of the arts, ACA promotes public debate in various national, state and local forums; communicates as a publisher of books, journals, *Vantage Point* magazine and *ACA UpDate*; provides information services through its extensive arts education, policy and management library; and has as its key policy issues arts education, the needs of individual artists, private-sector initiatives, and international cultural relations.

Murray Charles Pfister
Mrs. Richard S. Reynolds III
W. Ann Reynolds
David Rockefeller, Jr.
Henry C. Rogers
Mrs. Paul Schorr III
Gerard Schwarz
Mrs. Alfred R. Shands
David E. Skinner
Elton B. Stephens
Mr. John Straus
Mrs. Richard L. Swig
Allen M. Turner
Esther Wachtell
Vivian M. Warfield
Mrs. Gerald H. Westby
Mrs. Pete Wilson

Special Counsel
Jack G. Duncan

MAJOR CONTRIBUTORS

GOLDEN BENEFACTORS ($75,000 and up)
American Telephone &
   Telegraph Company
Gannett Foundation
Southwestern Bell

BENEFACTORS ($50,000-$74,999)
Aetna Life & Casualty
   Company
National Endowment for the
   Arts
Southwestern Bell

SUSTAINERS ($25,000-$49,999)
Robert H. Ahmanson
American Re-Insurance Co.
Mr. and Mrs. Jack S.
   Blanton, Sr.
The Coca-Cola Company

Eleanor Naylor Dana Trust
Philip Morris Companies, Inc.
The Reed Foundation
Sears, Roebuck & Co.
Elton B. Stephens
Mr. and Mrs. Richard L. Swig

SPONSORS ($15,000-$24,999)
Bozell, Jacobs, Kenyon &
   Eckhardt
Geraldine R. Dodge Foundation
Exxon Corporation
General Motors Corporation
IBM Corporation
Ruth Lilly
Merrill Lynch, Pierce, Fenner,
   & Smith Incorporated
Metropolitan Life Foundation
Mutual Benefit Life
Peat Marwick & Main
Rockefeller Foundation
The San Francisco Foundation
Reverend and Mrs. Alfred R.
   Shands III
Mr. John Straus

PATRONS ($10,000-$14,999)
American International
   Corporation
American International Group,
   Inc.
Ashland Oil, Inc.
Mr. and Mrs. Frederick
   Dupree, Jr.
Equitable Life Assurance
   Society
Toni K. Goodale
The Irvine Company
Susan R. Kelly
N.W. Ayer, Inc.
Mrs. Charles Peebler
Murray Charles Pfister

The Prudential Foundation
Mr. and Mrs. Paul Schorr III

DONORS ($5,000-$9,999)
The Allstate Foundation
American Stock Exchange, Inc.
Ameritech
The Arts, Education and
    Americans, Inc.
Atlantic Richfield Company
Batus, Inc.
Bell Atlantic
Mary Duke Biddle Foundation
Boeing Company
Chase Manhatten Bank
CIGNA Corporation
Dayton Hudson Foundation
Joseph Drown Foundation
Jeaneane B. Duncan
Mr. and Mrs. Frederick
    Dupree, Jr.
Federated Investors, Inc.
The First Boston Corporation
Ford Motor Company Fund
Gannett Outdoor
Goldman, Sachs & Company
Mr. and Mrs. John Hall
David H. Harris
Louis Harris & Associates
The Hartford Courant
Howard S. Kelberg
The Joe and Emily Lowe
    Foundation, Inc.
Lewis Manilow
MBIA, Inc.
Mobil Fondation, Inc.
Morgan Guaranty Trust
    Company
J.P. Morgan Securities
Morrison-Knudsen Corporation
New York Times Company
    Foundation

Pacific Telesis Group
General Dillman A. Rash
RJR Nabisco, Inc.
Mr. David Rockefeller, Jr.
Henry C. Rogers
Mr. and Mrs. LeRoy Rubin
Shell Companies Foundation
David E. Skinner
Allen M. Turner
Warner Lambert Company
Whirlpool Foundation
Xerox Corporation

CONTRIBUTORS ($2,000–$4,999)
Abbott Laboratories
Alcoa Foundation
Allied Corporation
American Electric Power
    Company, Inc.
American Express Foundation
Mr. and Mrs. Curtis L. Blake
Gerald D. Blatherwick
Edward Block
Borg-Warner Co.
Mrs. Eveline Boulafendis
Donald L. Bren
Bristol-Myers Fund
Mr. and Mrs. Martin Brown
C.W. Shaver
Terri and Timothy Childs
Chevron USA, Inc.
Robert Cochran
Mr. and Mrs. Hill Colbert
Mr. and Mrs. Donald G.
    Conrad
BarbaraLee Diamonstein-
    Spielvogel
Mr. and Mrs. Charles W.
    Duncan, Jr.
Mrs. George Dunklin
Eastman Kodak Company

Emerson Electric Co.
Ethyl Corporation
GFI/KNOLL International
  Foundation
Thomas M. Giardini
Donald R. Greene
Eldridge C. Hanes
Mr. and Mrs. Irving B. Harris
Ruth and Skitch Henderson
Henry Kates
John Kilpatrick
Kraft, Inc.
Mr. Robert Krissel
Marsh & McLennan Companies
Mr. and Mrs. John B. McCory
The Monsanto Fund
Robert M. Montgomery, Jr.
Velma V. Morrison
New York Life Foundation
Overbrook Foundation
Mr. and Mrs. Thomas Pariseleti
Procter & Gamble Fund
Raytheon Company
Mr. and Mrs. Richard S.
  Reynolds III
Judith and Ronald S. Rosen
Rubbermaid, Inc.
Sara Lee Corporation
Frank Saunders
Union Pacific Foundation
Mrs. Gerald H. Westby
Westinghouse Electric Fund
Mrs. Thomas Williams, Jr.
Betty Bentsen Winn

FRIENDS ($1,000–$1,999)
Morris J. Alhadeff
Mr. and Mrs. Arthur G.
  Altschul
AmSouth Bank N.A.
Archer Daniels Midland Co.
Mr. Wallace Barnes
Bell South

Mr. Stephen Belth
Mr. and Mrs. Evan Beros
Biney & Smith
T. Winfield Blackwell
Houston Blount
Bowne of Atlanta, Inc.
William A. Brady, M.D.
Alan Cameros
Mr. and Mrs. George Carey
Chris Carson
Mrs. George P. Caulkins
Mr. Campbell Cawood
Mrs. Jay Cherniack
Chesebrough-Pond's Inc.
Chrysler Corporation Fund
Citizens and Southern
  Corporation
David L. Coffin
Mr. and Mrs. Marshall Cogan
Thomas B. Coleman
Cooper Industries
Mrs. Howard Cowan
Cowles Charitable Trust
John G. Crosby
Mrs. Crittenden Currie
David L. Davies
Eugene C. Dorsey
Mrs. Frederick Dupree
Ronald and Hope Eastman
EBSCO Industries, Inc.
Mrs. Hubert Everist
Mary and Kent Frates
Stephanie French
Frederick P. Furth
Mr. and Mrs. Edward Gaylord
Dr. and Mrs. John M. Gibbons
Mrs. and Mrs. Edward Gildea
Lee Gillespie
Mr. and Mrs. Robert C.
  Graham, Jr.
Mr. and Mrs. W. Grant
  Gregory

Bernice Grossman and Stephen
  Belth
R. Philip Hanes, Jr.
Mr. and Mrs. Joseph Helman
Edward I. Herbst
Admiral and Mrs. B.R. Inman
Mrs. Lyndon B. Johnson
Mr. and Mrs. Thomas Jolly
Alexander Julian
L. Paul Kassouf
Mrs. Albert Kerry
Shane Kilpatrick
Mrs. Roy A. Kite
Mrs. James Knapp
Henry Kohn
Mrs. C.L. Landen, Jr.
Fred Lazarus IV
Thomas B. Lemann
Robert Leys
Ellen Liman
Dr. and Mrs. James L. Lodge
Mrs. Robert Lorton
Mr. and Mrs. I.W. Marks
Mr. and Mrs. Peter Marzio
Mr. and Mrs. James W.
  McElvany
Florri D. McMillan
Tim McReynolds
Mrs. Michale A. Miles
Mr. and Mrs. Reese L. Milner II
Wendy and Alan Mintz
Mr. and Mrs. George Mitchell
Mr. and Mrs. Robert Mosbacher
Sondra G. Myers
Mr. and Mrs. William G.
  Pannill
Pantone, Inc.
Diane Parker
Mr. and Mrs. R. Scott Pastrick

Mr. and Mrs. Harry Phillips, Jr.
Phillips Petroleum Foundation
Mr. and Mrs. John Powers
W. Ann Reynolds
William T. Reynolds
Mrs. Kay Riordan-Steuerwald
Mr. and Mrs. William A.
  Roever
Mrs. William A. Schreyer
Security Pacific
Dr. James H. Semans
Marie Walsh Sharpe Art
  Foundation
Gary F. Sherlock
Dorman and Shirley Shockley
Richard K. Smucker
Sotheby's North America
Thomas K. Standish
Mr. and Mrs. Stephen D.
  Susman
Tandy Corporation
Mr. and Mrs. Thomas R.
  Tellefsen
Textron Charitable Trust
Gerald Thornton
Mr. and Mrs. Thomas
  Troubridge
Mr. Gordon Ulmer
Mrs. John E. Velde, Jr.
Esther Wachtell
Mark Weiner
Frederick Weisman
Mrs. William F. Whitfield
Lawrence A. Wien
Elaine Percy Wilson
Mr. and Mrs. Wallace S. Wilson
Mrs. R. Dan Winn
Mr. and Mrs. William T. Young

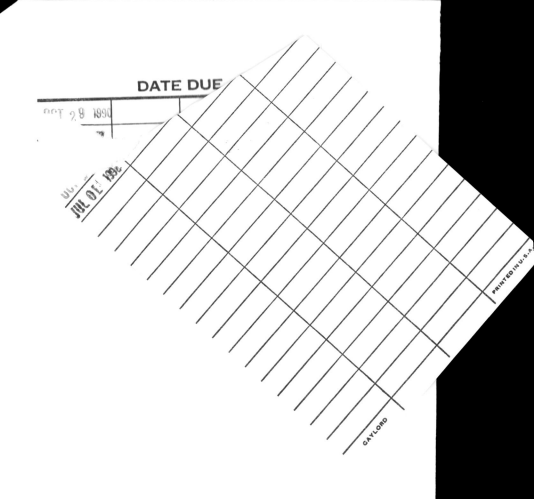

DATE DUE